# E. M. Bounds

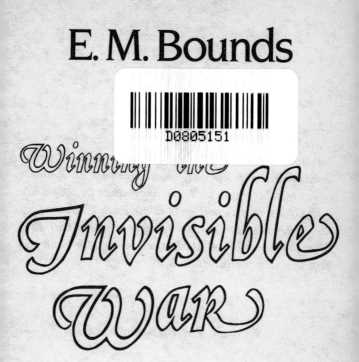

# Winning the Invisible War

Formerly: Satan: His Personality,
Power, And Overthrow

## PUBLISHER'S NOTE

*E.M. Bounds has taken a difficult subject and written a book that is not only challenging but enjoyable. In editing this book, we have maintained Dr. Bounds' delightful and unusual style while adding clarity for the modern reader. It is our prayer that you will discover and implement the principles in this book to help you win the invisible war.*

## Winning The Invisible War

Copyright © 1984 by Whitaker House
Printed in the United States of America
ISBN: 0-88368-145-5

# CONTENTS

# FOREWORD

If you had lived during the early years of the twentieth century, you could have visited a small town and witnessed a most unusual sight. You could have seen Dr. Bounds walking the streets carrying his manuscripts. They would have been written on the backs of old, used envelopes and tied with twine string. He was looking for someone who would undertake to prepare them for publication. Dr. Bounds was continually asking his friends to pray that God would raise up a man who would put his writings into print.

Claudius Lysias Chilton, a scholarly friend of Dr. Bounds, said, "There is no man on earth today except the present editor who would have accepted this mass of matter and devoted the time to give it to the world—a world that will not begin to realize the magnitude and expanse of the work until editor, compiler, and reviewers have been in eternity many ages."

We take this occasion to offer our heartfelt thanks to the friends who have helped to compile, revise, rewrite, and edit the printed and unprinted works of Dr. Bounds. We thank Rev. Robert O. Smith of Gainesville, Georgia, for introducing him to us in 1905 and insisting that we needed this apostolic man to teach us to pray and preach the Word.

I here submit a few brief statements from Dr. Bounds' letters to me just before he died. These show his views of Satan before he was taken out of the enemy's reach forever.

"I am trying to give myself more and more to prayer. Our only hope is in God. I do sympathize with you and pray for you and hold you in loving affection. Rejoice that you are well situated. God save you from your buffeting devil. The devil is a great help heavenward. The worse agents he has the better we will get on.

"Pray more and more; keep at the four a.m. hour. God will be for it; the devil against it. Press on, you can't pray too much; you may pray too little. The devil will compromise with you to pray as the common standard, on going to bed, and a little prayer in the morning. Hell will be full if we don't do better for God than that. Pray, pray, pray, pray always, rejoice evermore, pray without ceasing, in everything give thanks."

I hope that many souls will be edified and made holier and more devout by the reading of this book. I pray that God will receive additional glory when Bounds' complete works have been given to a needy world.

Homer W. Hodge
Brooklyn, New York

Chapter One

# WHO IS THE INVISIBLE ENEMY?

*"How art thou fallen from heaven, O Lucifer, son of the morning! how art thou cut down to the ground, which didst weaken the nations! For thou hast said in thine heart, I will ascend into heaven, I will exalt my throne above the stars of God: I will sit also upon the mount of the congregation, in the sides of the north: I will ascend above the heights of the clouds; I will be like the most High. Yet thou shalt be brought down to hell, to the sides of the pit"*—Isaiah 14:12-15.

The Bible does not give us any direct statements concerning the genesis of the devil. It gives us no indication of his birth and no description of his creation. The Bible is only concerned with the devil as he has part in the great crises of man's history. There are only occasional glimpses of him in his work of ruin and death. These glimpses put his acts in striking contrast and opposition to the works and aims of Christ. These inferences indicate an original purity, a high relationship to God, and a heavenly character and conduct. He was and is the head of the angels who left their first estate.

Peter gives the angels' fall as one of the events which illustrate God's justice, its certainty, and fearfulness. He says, "God spared not the angels that sinned, but cast them down to hell, and delivered them into chains of darkness, to be reserved unto judgment" (2 Peter 2:4). Jude speaks about the same order of God's inflexible wrath when he tells us that "the angels which kept not their first estate, but left their own habitation, he hath reserved in everlasting chains under darkness unto the judgment of the great day" (Jude 6).

The Revelation of John adds its testimony to this fact: "And there was war in heaven: Michael and his angels fought against the dragon; and the dragon fought and his angels, and prevailed not; neither was there place found any more in heaven. And the great dragon was cast out, that old serpent, called the Devil, and Satan, which deceiveth the whole world: he was cast out into the earth, and his angels were cast out with him" (Revelation 12:7-9).

### Unveiling The Enemy

We can approach the Word of God with the assurance that we will find traces of the devil's steps and the unfolding of his conduct. God's Word tells us of his evil schemes which have eclipsed so much of earth's brightness and spoiled so much of its promise and hope.

We must have a childlike spirit of trust and lay aside "all filthiness and superfluity of naughtiness, and receive with meekness the engrafted word" (James 1:21). Then we will find satisfaction and illumination of the truth. However, we will not satisfy our curiosity or find illumination in the fine points of philosophy. But we will find satisfaction and illumination in all things which pertain to the highest truth for the thoughtful, trustful, and prayerful mind.

In the Bible we have the facts and history of man's redemption. Other worlds and other beings are brought into prominence in light of redemption's purposes and plans. These revealed facts, whether incidental or essential, are to our faith what the facts of nature are to the biology student. They must shape theories and settle opinions. They must not be set aside. Reason must not ignore or reject them, but must lay them as the solid foundations of all investigation, the basis of every hypothesis. These Bible facts demand our faith, though we may not be able to reach out into the unknown regions where harmony reigns.

The Word of God brings clearly to light the unseen world, its persons, places, facts, and history. These are revealed not in minute detail, but with enough information to provoke thought and inspire faith.

## The Devil Revealed

The Bible does not enter into an argument to prove the person and being of God. It assumes His being and reveals His person and character. Without preface or introduction, the Bible brings

God before us in all His majesty and omnipotence. God is at the world's beginning, and He created the beginning of all things. "In the beginning God created the heavens and the earth" (Genesis 1:1). How sublime and inspiring is our first glimpse of God! God is revealed not by argument but by work. We learn what He is from what He does.

The revelation of the devil is the same. He is presented without introduction or ceremony as the evil one, a graduate in the school of deception and evil. The curtain is drawn and the chief actor is in full dress. A world is at stake, man is to be seduced, Eden is to be corrupted. No light is shed upon his past history. No knowledge is given of the school where he learned his evil trade. He was before earthly life. Eden does not date his birth. It is not the first chapter of his history or the first test of his hellish art.

We have no access to the archives of the past. Eden bounds our horizon, and the devil is there. Since that time, his history has run parallel with the human race. Man is the object of his schemes, his destructive devices, and his ambition. Earth is the favorite scene of his exploits. He is at the cradle of every baby, and he has much to do in shaping each person's character and determining his destiny.

The Bible is a revelation, not a philosophy or a poem, not a science. It reveals things and persons as they are, living and acting outside the range of earthly vision or natural discovery.

Bible revelations are not against reason but

10

above reason. They require the exercise of faith, man's highest faculty. The powers of reason are not able to discover these Bible facts. Yet, these facts are for reason's use, its light, strength, and higher elevation. But most essentially they are to form, nourish, and perfect faith.

## The Devil Is A Real Person

The Bible reveals the devil as a person—not a mere figure, not simply an influence. He is not only a personification, but a real person. In the eighth chapter of John, Christ is accusing the cruelty, falsehood, deceit, and hypocrisy of the Jews. Jesus says, "Ye are of your father the devil, and the lusts of your father ye will do. He was a murderer from the beginning, and abode not in the truth, because there is no truth in him" (John 8:44).

Many myths have gathered around the person of the devil throughout the ages. Much poetry, tradition, and even our fears have caricatured his person, exaggerated his character, and colored his conduct. But there is truth in regard to him, naked and simple truth.

There is much truth that needs to be learned about the devil, and no age needs the plain, unvarnished truth about him more than this generation. We need the light of that truth as a warning, as an incentive to vigilance, and an inspiration to effort. We need the knowledge about the enemy, his character, presence, and power in order to arouse men to action. This knowledge is vital to victory.

Many people deny the existence of Satan and his

influence in our lives. Would Christ have used such plain and solemn words repeatedly before His disciples and the Jews to encourage a lying superstition? To deny the reality of demon possession as recorded in the gospels is simply inconceivable.

## The Devil And His Angels

When the devil fell, others fell with him. This is what God's Word teaches us. We have no record of the number of these fallen spirits. In Ephesians these unseen foes are spoken of as "spiritual hosts," an uncounted, uncountable number (Ephesians 6:12, *R.S.V.*).

How innumerable they are, we cannot tell. The demoniac of Gadara was named "Legion because many devils were entered into him" (Luke 8:30). A legion was somewhat less than six thousand. Their number must be great because they are able to permit so many demons to possess one man; or allow seven to control one woman, as Mary Magdalene.

There is a statement in Revelation that the great red dragon with "his tail did draw the third part of the stars of heaven, and did cast them to the earth" (Revelation 12:4). This may be a reference to the fall of the angels and their number.

The Bible clearly states that the devil has a host of angelic followers who are ready and eager in their efforts to hurt man and defeat God's Kingdom on earth.

Chapter Two

# IDENTIFYING THE DEVIL'S PERSONALITY

*"(The devil). . .was a murderer from the beginning, and abode not in the truth, because there is no truth in him. When he speaketh a lie, he speaketh of his own: for he is a liar, and the father of it"*—John 8:44.

The devil is a personality with definite character. Character can give dignity and value to a person, or character can degrade the person. Character is the inner life of a person which forms action and shapes life. Character is a fountain—the head and stream of conduct.

However, character is often opposed to a person's reputation. Character is what we are. Reputation is what people think we are. The *real* and the *think so* are often two different worlds. It would be marvelous if reputation were based on character, if the real and the reputed were one. A bad reputation can be coupled with good character. Conversely, a good reputation can cover up bad character. Reputation is based on character. They are one. The devil's reputation is bad, because his character is worse.

The devil is a *created being*. He is therefore not self-existent or eternal, but limited and finite. There was a time when he was not, when he began to be. His creation was after the order of the angels. The angels were not the offspring of the family relationship. All the tender emotions, training, sweetness, and growth of infancy are unknown to them. The pains and joys of childbirth are not theirs. Each angel is created, not born. They are created directly and personally by God. As an angel, the devil was created good, doubtless very good. His purity as well as exaltation were sources of congratulation, wonderment, and praise in heaven.

The devil is a *positive character*. He wears disguises, but his objectives lie in only one direction. He is double-faced but never double-minded, never undecided, vague, or feeble in his purposes or ends. No irresolution, hesitancy, or aimless action ever spring from him.

The devil has character if not horns, because character is often harder and sharper than horns. Character is felt. We feel the devil. He orders and controls things. He is a great manager. He manages bad men and fallen angels. The devil is an indirect, sinister, low, and worldly manager.

## The Personality Of The Devil

Is Christ a person? He puts the devil in contrast to Himself as a great, mighty, wicked person who is the sower of all evil—as Christ is the sower of all good. "The field is the world; the good seed are the children of the Kingdom; but the tares are the children of the wicked one; the enemy that sowed them is the devil; the harvest is the end of the world; and the reapers are the angels" (Matthew 13:38,39).

Is Christ impersonal? Are the children of the Kingdom impersonal? Are the children of the wicked one impersonal? Are not Christ and the children of the Kingdom personal and persons? Are not the children of the wicked one and the devil personal and persons also?

In the Bible the personality of the devil is made a reality. He is not only the source of evil to others, but the embodiment of evil in a person. The Revised Standard Version makes this clear. The petition in the Lord's prayer, "Deliver us from evil," becomes personal, "Deliver us from *the evil one*" (Matthew 6:13). So we find Christ praying not only that His disciples should be delivered from evil, all evil, impersonal and general, but "that thou shouldst keep them from the *evil one*." (John 17:15).

The statement by John that "the whole world lieth in wickedness," becomes personal, for, in the Revised Standard Version, all wickedness concentrates in a person: "The whole world is in the power of the *evil one*" (1 John 5:19). Here, too, the devil is called the "evil one." Personality is attributed to him. Fatherhood is attributed to him because he is the father of all evil. He is the enemy of Jesus, destructive, active, crafty, cautious, and cowardly.

## The Prince of Evil

The devil and his angels are of a higher order than the fallen sons of Adam, by rank, order, and intelligence. The devil is called in the Bible a prince, a world ruler, "prince of this world" (John 12:31). He is designated as "the devil and his angels" (Matthew 25:41). He and they are held accountable for their sins. They are condemned for their revolt in leaving their "first estate" (Jude 6), the sphere for which they were created and in which they were originally placed by God.

This fact of their fall and all the other scriptural statements, direct and incidental, emphasize them as persons, living, acting, free, and accountable. They had a chief prince who organized all their movements. The fact that they were led by a wise and skilled leader is clear from all scriptural statements concerning the devil and his angels.

In 2 Corinthians 11:13, Paul says: "For such are false apostles, deceitful workers, transforming themselves into the apostles of Christ. And no marvel; for Satan himself is transformed into an angel of light. Therefore it is no great thing if his ministers also be transformed as the ministers of righteousness; whose end shall be according to their works." The statement "Satan himself" is an emphatic declaration of personality. He has ministers. An influence does not have ministers. Paul is writing about persons who are fraudulent and alluring. He introduces this great leader as the arch-imposter, the inspirer of all the fraud, hypocrisy, and error of his apostles who are as false as he is.

Jude has a statement which brings into view many personalities: "Likewise also these filthy dreamers defile the flesh, despise dominion, and speak evil of dignities. Yet Michael the archangel, when contending with the devil he disputed about the body of Moses, durst not bring against him a railing accusation, but said, The Lord rebuke thee" (Jude 1:8,9).

The "filthy dreamers" were persons. Moses was a great person. Michael an archangel was an actual being. The devil, what was he, if not a living, active personality?

## A High Dignitary

During Moses' time, the devil was contending with Michael, the highest angelic dignitary. Did the mighty archangel have to appeal for help against a mere influence, a shadowy, dreamy personification? This statement in Jude declares the devil to be a high dignitary, whose person and presence are not to be treated with dishonor or frivolity.

This statement in Peter gives further evidence of the fact that the devil is a person of high nobility. "The Lord knoweth how to deliver the godly out of temptation, and to reserve the unjust unto the day of judgment to be punished: But chiefly them that walk after the flesh in the lust of uncleanness,

17

and despise government. Presumptuous are they, self-willed, they are not afraid to speak evil of dignities. Whereas angels, which are greater in power and might, bring not railing accusation against them before the Lord. But these, as natural brute beasts, made to be taken and destroyed, speak evil of the things that they understand not; and shall utterly perish in their own corruption'' (2 Peter 2:9-12).

Note how James puts the mightiest beings in contrast and opposition: ''Submit yourselves therefore to God. Resist the devil, and he will flee from you. Draw nigh to God and He will draw nigh to you'' (James 4:7,8). Why such a combination and contrast? Is God not a living personality? How can we then reduce the devil to a mere influence? This passage teaches a personal devil as surely as a personal God.

Why are God and the devil spoken of in a similar manner in Peter's urgent exhortation? ''Humble yourselves therefore under the mighty hand of God, that He may exalt you in due time: casting all your care upon him; for He careth for you. Be sober, be vigilant; because your adversary the devil, as a roaring lion, walketh about, seeking whom he may devour'' (1 Peter 5:6-8). Why cast all care on Him? Why be sober and vigilant? ''Your adversary'' can be no less than an actual being against whom the Christian has to be armed with God's power.

''Your adversary!'' Hate and destruction are his weapons. Can he be less than a person? The devil is "walking about like a roaring lion," strong, full of passions, and deadly hate! Can anything less than a being of fiery passion and infernal power fulfill this divine portrait?

To Peter, the existence and personality of this powerful adversary had a sad demonstration in his own experience. The words were still on his conscience, heart, and memory. "Simon, behold, Satan hath desired to have you, that he may sift you as wheat" (Luke 22:31).

## Jesus And The Devil

In the instructions given in the Sermon on the Mount about swearing, affirmations, and conversation, Jesus says, "Let your communication be, Yea, yea; Nay, nay: for whatsoever is more than these cometh of evil" (Matthew 5:37).

Under the powerful operations of the cross and the Spirit, as well as the restraining influences of the gospel, why has evil not been driven from the earth? It is because of the mighty personality and executive ability of the devil.

We find many references, hints, and reminders of the power and personality of the devil coming out in the ministry of Christ. The name "devil" invests him with an infamous personality and clothes him with all the deceit, craft, and cruelty attached to that name. By the name "Satan," Christ puts him as the adversary of God and man. By designating him as "the prince of this world," Christ recognizes Satan's royal power and ruling authority over evil in this world. The devil's ability to affect the body with sickness is not merely hinted at, but taken for granted in the gospels.

The conflict between the devil and Jesus is seen in the Lord's prayer. It is that perfect and universal prayer which Jesus puts in the heart and lips of His people. We have seen, according to the Revised Standard Version, this petition of conflict, peril, warning, and safety: "Deliver us from the evil one" (Matthew 6:13). Evil is comparatively harmless, feeble, and inert without the presence of its mighty inspirer. Deliverance from the devil is deliverance from the many evils of which he is the source and inspiration.

## Warnings About The Devil

In the sixth chapter of Ephesians, the Christian is presented as a soldier in character, armor, conduct, and courage. Because of the devil's power, and because the Christian's warfare is mainly against him, we are urged to: "Put on the whole armour of God, that ye may be able to stand against the wiles of the devil. For we wrestle not against flesh and blood, but against principalities, against powers, against the rulers of the darkness of this world, against spiritual wickedness in high places" (Ephesians 6:11,12).

The Christian's comfort as administered by Paul in the sixteenth chapter of Romans is not only the impartation of, "The grace of the Lord Jesus Christ be with you," but also, "And the God of peace shall bruise Satan under your feet shortly" (verse 20).

Peter's vital exhortation has a double imperative in it, not only the "casting all our care on God," but a loud and urgent call to watch and pray. "Be sober, be vigilant; because your adversary the devil, as a roaring lion, walketh about, seeking whom he may devour" (1 Peter 5:6-8).

Peter recognized in the deadly crime of Ananias and Sapphira the hand of Satan, "Ananias, why hath Satan filled thine heart to lie to the Holy Ghost, and to keep back part of the price of the land?" (Acts 5:3).

The warning which Christ sends to the church at Smyrna to prepare for tribulation involves the personality and power of the devil. "Fear none of those things which thou shalt suffer: behold, the devil shall cast some of you into prison, that ye may be tried; and ye shall have tribulation ten days: be thou faithful unto death, and I will give thee a crown of life" (Revelation 2:10).

The explanation of the parable of the tares puts the wickedness, personality, and power of the devil in contrast with Christ. "The field is the world; the good seed are the children of the kingdom; but the tares are the children of the wicked one; The enemy that sowed them is the devil; the harvest is the end of the world; and the reapers are the angels" (Matthew 13:39).

## The Devil's Evil Work

The defense of Christ against the Pharasee's charge of violating the Sabbath exposes the devil in his work of evil: "And ought not this woman, being a daughter of Abraham, whom Satan hath bound, lo, these eighteen years, be loosed from this bond on the sabbath day?" (Luke 13:16).

It is said about Judas, "And supper being ended, the devil having now put into the heart of Judas Iscariot, Simon's son, to betray Him" (John 13:2). This is a statement not of an influence or a personification, but of a personality outside of Judas, making suggestions to him and urging him on to his act of hypocrisy. This suggestion is strictly in keeping with the character of the devil.

"And after the sop Satan entered into him. Then said Jesus unto him, That thou doest, do quickly" (John 13:27). This act is greatly advanced in power of action and influence compared with Satan's work in the Garden! There he used a serpent as his instrument. Here he uses a man, a chosen, trusted apostle.

"The messenger of Satan," says Paul, "to buffet me" (2 Corinthians 12:7). The exalted revelation and experience of the person and power of Christ are closely followed by the revelation and experience of the person and power of the devil.

Christ explains the fearful doom that awaits the wicked at the time of judgment: "Then shall He say also unto them on the left hand, Depart from Me, ye cursed, into everlasting fire, prepared for the devil and his angels" (Matthew 25:41). The final doom of Satan is revealed in these words, "And the devil that deceived them was cast into the lake of fire and brimstone, where the beast and the false prophets are, and shall be tormented day and night for ever and ever" (Revelation 20:10).

These extracts are not simply arguments to prove the existence or personality of the devil. Instead, they are logical, conclusive references to a being whose reality is taken for granted, universally accepted, and thoroughly believed by Christ and the early apostles.

An exception to this would be the person who professes to accept God's Word and yet does not believe in the existence of the devil. This would be a great breach both in logic and faith. It would be the same as if a person accepted the play of "Macbeth" yet failed to recognize the person or existence of Lady Macbeth, whose character forms the plan and nature of the entire plot.

## Christ's View Of The Devil

Christ's encounters with those who were possessed of devils illustrate His constant recognition of them as personal beings. He recognizes their distinct individuality. He talks to them and commands them as persons. They know Christ, confess His divinity, bow to His authority, and obey, however unwillingly, His commands.

Jesus makes the clear distinction between the *human personality* possessed by the devil and *the personality of the devil* who holds possession. In his eyes, they are *two distinct persons*.

The exercising of this distinction gave a severe blow to Satan's kingdom. At the return and report of the seventy disciples, they said, "Even the devils are subject unto us through Thy name." Jesus exclaimed, "I beheld Satan as lightning fall from heaven," and then amid their ecstasy and His joy, He renewed their commission: "Behold, I give unto you power to tread on serpents and scorpions, and over all the power of the enemy: and nothing shall by any means hurt you. Notwithstanding in this rejoice not, that the spirits are subject unto you; but rather rejoice, because your names are written in heaven" (Luke 10:17-20).

"Over all the power of the enemy." The devil is the enemy of Christ and of man. Jesus gave His disciples power over all the devil's power. To Christ the devil was a very real person. He recognized his personality, felt and acknowledged his power, abhorred his character, and warred against his kingdom.

# Chapter Three

# RECOGNIZING THE PRINCE OF THIS WORLD

*"Jesus answered and said, This voice came not because of me, but for your sakes. Now is the judgment of this world: now shall the prince of this world be cast out. And I, if I be lifted up from the earth, will draw all men unto me"*— John 12:30-32.

The Holy Spirit is the substitute, representative, and successor of Jesus Christ. To the Holy Spirit was committed this work of breaking the deadly power of the world by breaking the power of its prince. Jesus reminded His disciples that the devil, who occupied the royal position as the world's prince, was already judged, condemned, and sentenced.

"Nevertheless, I tell you the truth; It is expedient for you that I go away: for if I go not away, the Comforter will not come unto you; but if I depart, I will send Him unto you. And when He is come, He will reprove the world of sin, and of righteousness, and of judgment: Of sin, because they believe not on Me; Of righteousness, because I go to My Father, and ye see Me no more; Of judgment, because the prince of this world is judged'' (John 16:7-11). Satan may be the prince of this world, but there is an awful doom awaiting him because he is the author of unbelief, sin, and unrighteousness.

## What Is Satan's Position?

In these declarations of Jesus Christ, we have the clear revelation of what the devil is in his relationship to the world as a prince and ruler. We understand why the world is so alien to God, to God's Son, and to His cause. We understand how attachment to the world creates estrangement and bitter enmity to God. This happens because the world's beauty and charms reflect the opposition of the devil to God. The world is the sensuous harlot with her snares of death and hell.

The devil is recognized by Jesus Christ to be the prince of this world, not lawfully, but in its rebellion against God. The devil is not to be submitted to, but to be renounced as a lawless criminal, dethroned as a usurper, and conquered as a rebel. The Son of God is given this mission: to dethrone and conquer the devil.

We see how readily Jesus Christ acknowledges the position and power of the devil. When He speaks of the devil, He equates him with the world. The stroke of the Son of God falls on both: "Now is the judgment of this world; now shall the prince of this world be cast out. And I, if I be

lifted up, will draw all men to Me'' (John 12:31).
The world is condemned by the power of the
cross.

## The Power Of The Cross

The sweet, attractive powers of the cross dis-
solve the fatal fascinations of the world. The
power of that same cross casts out from his ruling
throne the prince of this world.

Christ affirms the devil's high position, but also
signs and seals his destiny and doom. ''God
anointed Jesus of Nazareth with the Holy Ghost
and with power: who went about doing good, and
healing all that were oppressed of the devil; for
God was with Him'' (Acts 10:38).

Again the Son of God recognizes the position
which the devil holds as crowned prince by the
world's powers. His presence quiets the Son of
God. Man's words are not to be victors in this
conflict. Jesus used God's words in the time of
temptation. With these He broke the power of
Satan's assault and defeated his evil intentions. But
Jesus left him still a sovereign with his kingly
crown.

The Son of God remained silent at the devil's
approach. The cross, its deep humiliation, bitter
agony, its defeat and despair——it took all these to
lift the crown from Satan's brow and bring his
throne down to dust and ashes. The adorable Son
of God saw ''the travail of His soul'' and was satisfied (Isaiah 53:11).

Jesus saw what it would cost Him and what it

would cost every son of heaven to discrown that prince. Because of this, He lapsed into a solemn silence, the prestige of His victory. "Hereafter I will not talk much with you: for the prince of this world cometh, and hath nothing in Me" (John 14:30).

Chapter Four

# WHAT IS THE DEVIL'S BUSINESS?

*"Then was Jesus led up of the Spirit into the wilderness to be tempted of the devil. And when he had fasted forty days and forty nights, he was afterward an hungred. And when the tempter came to him, he said, If thou be the Son of God, command that these stones be made bread. But he answered and said, It is written, Man shall not live by bread alone, but by every word that proceedeth out of the mouth of God. Then the devil taketh him up into the holy city, and setteth him on a pinnacle of the temple, and saith unto him, If thou be the Son of God, cast thyself down: for it is written, He shall give his angels charge concerning thee. . . Jesus said unto him, It is written again, Thou shalt not tempt the Lord thy God. Again the devil taketh him up into an exceeding high mountain, and sheweth him all the kingdoms of the world, and the glory of them; and saith unto him, All these things will I give thee, if thou wilt fall down and worship me. Then saith Jesus unto him, Get thee hence, Satan:*

*for it is written, Thou shalt worship the Lord thy God, and him only shalt thou serve. Then the devil leaveth him, and, behold, angels came and ministered unto him''*—Matthew 4:1-11.

If there is any praise to always being busy, the devil may claim that praise, for he is always very busy. But his character does not spring from his faith. His faith makes him tremble, his character makes him a devil.

The devil is a very busy character. He does a big business, a very ugly business, but he does it well, that is, as well as an ugly business can be done. He has lots of experience, big brains, a black heart, great force, tireless energy, and is of great influence and great character. All his immense resources and powers are used for evil purposes. Only evil inspires his activities and energies. He never moves to relieve or bless. He is a stranger to benevolent deeds and compassionate feeling.

Satan's history antedates the history of man. He and his angels are the only beings who have experienced heaven, earth, and hell. These three places are familiar to him. He has walked the streets of heaven side by side with its purest and best. He has felt the thrill of its purest joys. He knows the bitterest anguish of hell and has felt its keenest flames.

He does a big business on earth. He is a prince and a leader. Men and devils are his agents. The elements of nature are often corrupted by him from their beneficial purposes and forced to destroy. He is busy tempting men to do evil. He has lots of experience in this business and is very adept at it. By his schemes, sin seems to lose its sinfulness, the world is clothed with double charms, and self is given twice the force. He turns faith into fanaticism and love into hate.

## The Devil's Business

A spiritual character can work through other agencies or directly on the human spirit. Satan infuses thoughts, makes suggestions, and does it so deftly that we do not know their origin. He tempted Eve to take the forbidden fruit. He put it into David's mind to number Israel, thereby provoking the wrath of God. He influenced Ananias and Sapphira to lie to God.

Peter's yielding to presumption was instigated by Satan. Judas' betrayal was from the same poisonous source. The temptation of Christ was a typical masterpiece of Satan's craft. He tried to dissuade our Lord from God's purposes by showing Him his power to present alternatives with great persuasive logic.

Satan is blasphemous, arrogant, and presumptuous. He slanders God to men and infuses into their minds distorted thoughts about God. He intensifies their hatred and inflames their prejudice against Him. He leads them to deny God's existence and to misrepresent His character, thereby destroying the foundations of faith and all true worship.

Satan does all he can by insinuation and accusa-

tion to blacken saintly character and lower God's
estimate of the good. He is the vilest of maligners,
the most vicious and artful of slanderers. Goodness is the target of his constant attack. He says
nothing good about the good, nothing bad about
the bad.

Satan is always at church before the preacher is
in the pulpit or a member in the pew. He comes to
hinder the sower, to impoverish the soil, or to
corrupt the seed. He uses these tactics only when
courage and faith are in the pulpit, and when zeal
and prayer are in the pew. But if dead ritualism or
live liberalism are in the pulpit, he does not
attend because they are no danger to him.

### Satan's Tools Of The Trade

Christ expressly declared that some sickness, at
least, was directly inflicted by Satan. The devil
goes about to do evil and oppress men. At every
point he is the antagonist of Him who went about
doing good and healing all who were oppressed of
the devil. In some way he acquired the power of
death and created in men a fearful bondage to it.
Through death, Christ works to destroy him who
had the power of death, that is, the devil.

The devil puts a thorn in Paul's flesh and makes
a special effort to acquire Peter's loyalty. He
directs the whirlwind, kindles the fire, and orders
the disease which devastates Job and his property.
He arms the thieving Chaldeans and Sabines
against Job and gets control of his wife. He directs
the various offices of his empire to ruin this one

saint. He will wreck an empire at any time to secure a soul.

Satan sows the tares in the wheat, the bad among the good, bad thoughts among good thoughts. All kinds of evil seed are sown by him in the harvest fields of earth. He is always trying to make the good bad and the bad worse. He fills the mind of Judas, and he inflames and hurries him on to his infamous purpose. He fills Peter with an arrogant pride which tries to inject human views into the purpose of Christ instead of God's purpose.

The devil goes about as fierce, as resolute, and as strong as a lion, intent only to destroy. He is restrained by no sentiments which soften and move human or divine hearts. He has no pity and no sympathy. He is great, but only great in evil. He has a great intellect, but he is driven and inspired by a vicious and cruel heart.

## The Temptation Of Christ

At the threshold of Christ's ministry, He is met with temptation by the devil. The historical account of the situation presents the devil as a spiritual person. He is the head and embodiment of all evil, making a fierce and protracted assault on the Son of God. We are not informed as to what form he assumed in order to veil the treachery and wickedness of his attack.

The temptation of Christ is noted as one of the preliminary and pivotal facts of His ministry. It cannot be considered a vision any more than can His baptism, the descent of the Spirit, His wilderness trip, or His fasting. It was not an influence tempting Christ. The whole transaction forbids such a conclusion. "Jesus. . .was led of the Spirit into the wilderness to be tempted of the devil" (Matthew 4:1). The devil came to Him and the devil left Him, and then "the angels came and ministered to Him" (verse 11).

In this temptation, the methods, hypocrisy, and craft of the devil are seen. He comes to the weak, exhausted Son of God with an air of concern. How innocent is Satan's suggestion that Jesus use His power to relieve His hunger! What could be more permissable than to use His spiritual power for physical purposes? How often is it done? Whenever faith is used to serve the natural, the source is always evil.

It is man living for bread alone that makes the temporal become priority. The secular and worldly take on supreme importance. Faith becomes secondary— subservient to money and business. The heavenly is used for the earthly, the spiritual for the natural. We become more intent on daily food than on daily grace, eyeing the seen more than the unseen.

That is the devil's main business—to materialize religion, to get man to live for bread alone, to make earth bigger than heaven. Time is more intriguing than eternity. What a fearful conflict is being carried on in that quiet wilderness between the fainting Son of God and Satan. It is a struggle between the earthly and the heavenly, between God's religion and the devil's religion!

## The Points Of Conflict

The conflict surges around three points: the fleshly, the presumptuous, and the worldly. This little circle holds all the shapes and forms of temptation—all the crafty devices, all the hidden depths, all the glittering seductions which Satan has devised to swerve men from the allegiance which faith demands.

The devil's assault on Christ is in striking contrast with his temptation to beguile Eve. It is also in striking contrast with the fearful ordeal through which he tried Job's integrity. Satan casts no suspicion on God's goodness as he did with Eve. He causes no terrific, consuming sorrow as he did in Job's case. Instead, everything is friendly, sympathetic, and inviting.

The second temptation includes the fanatical presumption of overheated zeal and brainless devotion. Satan uses all the methods of sensational and abnormal religious practices. He tempts Jesus to take the shortcut by which the principles of genuine faith are set aside and superficial substitutes are brought in to make faith more attractive and popular. Presumption seeks to take man-devised methods, which are easy, sentimental, and material, instead of God's lowly way of godly sorrow, strict self-denial, and prayerful surrender.

The last temptation involves the world with its kingdoms and its glory. These are the rewards for devotion to Satan and worship of the devil—who is the world's god. How the devil massed all his forces! Religion was invoked. The world and the flesh all conspired, under Satan's power, to tempt the Son of God.

The reluctance with which the pure Son of God went unto this close conflict with Satan is seen in Mark's statement: "And immediately the Spirit driveth Him into the wilderness" (1:12). Nothing can warp this statement into a mere influence. It is history—plain, simple, documented fact. Without a doubt or figure of speech, the Bible clearly stamps the whole transaction with personality.

"Then was Jesus led up of the Spirit into the wilderness to be tempted of the devil" (Matthew 4:1). "And He was there in the wilderness forty days, tempted of Satan; and was with the wild beasts; and the angels ministered unto Him" (Mark 1:13). "Then the devil leaveth Him, and, behold, angels came and ministered unto Him" (Matthew 4:11). These are not figures of speech, but the narrative of a transaction and of persons engaged in the transaction. The wilderness and the fasting are literal. The beings are all literal, the wild beasts, the angels, Jesus, and the devil.

The conflict of Jesus with Satan is not incidental, accidental, or casual. But it is essential and vital. Satan held man and man's world in subjection. They had fallen into his hands and were held by him in bondage and ruled by him with desperate power.

The record has been made, "And when the devil had ended all the temptation, he departed from Him for a season" (Luke 4:13).

# The Agony In The Garden

The season has ended and Satan is back again as though he had brought seven other spirits more wicked than himself. Gethsemane is the sum of the devil's most maddened and desperate methods. The disguises are off. He appears there as he really is. It is a rare thing to get a clear, true light on the devil. He assumes so many roles, acts so many parts, wears so many disguises.

In the garden of Gethsemane, we see him in life-size form. The air is heavier by his breath, the night is darker by his shadow, the ground is colder and his chill is on it. Judas is falser still, and Peter is more cowardly, because Satan is there.

On the threshold of Gethsemane, Jesus exclaims, "My soul is exceeding sorrowful, even unto death" and He began to be grieved and very heavy (Matthew 26:38). Why? Because "this is your hour and the power of darkness" (Luke 22:53). Why? Because "now is the judgment of this world: now shall the prince of this world be cast out" (John 12:31). Everything is silent and there is an air of dread and horror. Why? "For the prince of this world cometh, and hath nothing in Me" (John 14:30).

In this situation, the devil's method with Christ is much different than it was in the wilderness. Then there was an assumed sympathy, the spirit of an inquirer, one anxious to relieve. In the wilderness, Satan offered the most pleasant, attractive, and satisfying ministries to the flesh. There was something of the gentleness of a lamb, the interest and sympathy of a friend. But now how that has changed in the garden! The lamb is transformed into a lion, a roaring lion who is maddened and desperate.

Jesus could not be seduced by the flesh or self or the world in the wilderness. He must be overwhelmed with dread and horror. His steadfastness must be overcome by weakness and fear. Satan comes to many saints in the fierceness and power of the lion when the gentle inducements fail.

Chapter Five

# SATAN'S MAIN TARGET

*Whom say ye that I am? And Simon Peter answered and said, Thou art the Christ, the Son of the living God. And Jesus answered and said unto him, Blessed art thou, Simon Barjona: for flesh and blood hath not revealed it unto thee, but my Father which is in heaven. And I say also unto thee, That thou art Peter, and upon this rock I will build my church; and the gates of hell shall not prevail against it"*—Matthew 16:15-18.

The devil is too wise and too lordly in ambition to confine his aims to the individual. Instead, he seeks to direct the policies and sway the governments of nations. In his passion for success, he goes out "to deceive the nations which are in the four quarters of the earth" (Revelation 20:8).

Satan is an expert in all the arts of deceit. He is an archangel in execution and he often succeeds in seducing the nations most loyal to Christ. He leads them into plans which pervert all scriptural principles. When the Church itself, the bride of Christ, is seduced from her purity, she degenerates into worldly ritualism.

The "gates of hell shall not prevail" against the Church (Matthew 16:18). This promise of our Lord stands against every Satanic device and assault. But this unchangeable word does not protect the Church from the devil's strategies which often pervert the aims of the Church and postpone the day of its final triumph.

The devil is a hydra-headed monster who is multifaceted in plans and wisdom as well as in atrocities. His supreme effort is to get control of the Church, not to destroy its organization, but to pervert its divine purpose. He does this in the most insidious way with no startling change and nothing to shock or alarm.

Sometimes revolutionary and destructive change is introduced under the disguise of a greater zeal for Christ's glory. It is often introduced by someone held in high esteem by the local church who is totally ignorant of the fact that the measure he is advocating is subversive.

## A False Sense Of Power

One of Satan's most perverse schemes is to establish a wrong estimate of church strength. If he can create false assessments of local church power; if he can press the material things to the forefront; if he can make these forces powerful in commands and influence, he has accomplished his purpose.

Under the law of Moses, the subversion of God's purposes and the substitutions of material forces were guarded against. The kings of Israel were warned against accumulation and reliance on material forces. King David was in violation of this law when he yielded to the temptation of Satan to number the people of Israel.

The third temptation of our Lord was intended to subvert the purposes of His Kingdom. Satan planned to do this by substituting material elements of strength for the spiritual.

This is one of the devil's most insidious and successful methods to deceive, divert, and deprave. He parades the most attractive material results. He praises the power of human planning before church leaders until they are dazzled and ensnared. Then the Church becomes thoroughly worldly while boasting of her spirituality. No deceiver is so artful in the diabolical trade of deception as Satan. As an angel of light, he leads a soul to death.

To mistake the true power of the Church's strength is to mistake the true character of the Church. When its character is changed, then all its efforts and aims are also changed. The strength of the Church lies in its devotion to God. All else is incidental and is not the source of its strength. But in worldly, popular language, a local church is called strong when its membership is large—when it has social position and financial resources. A church is thought to be powerful when ability, learning, and eloquence fill the pulpit—when the pews are filled by fashion, intelligence, money, and influence. An assumption of this kind is

41

worldly to the fullest extent.

## The Source Of True Power

The local church that defines its strength in this way is on the highway to apostasy. The strength of the Church does not consist of any or all of these things. The faith, holiness, and zeal of the Church are the elements of its power. Church strength does not consist in its numbers and its money, but in the holiness of its members. Church strength is not found in these worldly attachments or endowments, but in the endowment of the Holy Spirit on its members.

The most deadly symptom which can be seen in a church is the transferring of its strength from spiritual to material forces, from the Holy Spirit to the world. The power of God in the Church is the measure of its strength. This is the quality God looks for in a church. The power of the Holy Spirit gives the Church the ability to accomplish the purposes for which it was designed.

On the contrary, show us a church that is poor, illiterate, obscure, and unknown, but composed of praying people. They may not be men of power, wealth, or influence. Their families may not know one week where they are to get their bread for the next. But with them is "the hiding of God's power" (Habakkuk 3:4), and their influence will be felt for eternity. Wherever they go there is a fountain of light, and Christ in them is glorified and His Kingdom advanced. They are His chosen vessels of salvation who reflect His light.

Within the Church there are unmistakable signs that she has been blinded and caught by Satan's dazzling glare. The Church is being seriously affected by the material progress of the age. We have heard so much about prosperity and gazed on it so long that spiritual views no longer appeal to us. Everything must take on the rich quality, luxuriant growth, and magnificent appearance of the material, or else it seems beggarly. This is the most perilous condition the Church has to face. It happens when the meek and lowly fruits of holiness are discounted by the showy and worldly charms with which material success crowds the Church.

We must not yield to the flood. We must not for a moment, not the hundredth part of an inch, give place to the world. Holiness and devotion to God must be stressed in every way and at every point. The Church must be made to see this delusion and snare. This transference of strength from God to the world, this rejection of the Holy Spirit's endowment of "might and power" must be recognized as yielding to Satan. The Church, more and more, is inclined not only to disregard, but to despise, the elements of spiritual strength and set them aside for more impressive, worldly ideas.

## The Material Deception

We have been taught to regard the principles of church prosperity as only those items which can be seen in a statistical column. We seek to impress an age geared to the objectivity of secular facts and figures. However, the most vital spiritual conditions and gains cannot be reduced to figures. For this reason, they are left out of the numerical column, and, after a while, they are neither noted nor observed.

If we do not change our methods, our ideas concerning the strength of the local church will become worldly. No matter how imposing our material results may be, or how magnificent and prosperous the secular arm of the Church appears, we must go deeper than these for its strength. We must proclaim and reiterate with increased emphasis that the strength of the Church does not lie in these things.

These are the gilded delusions which we mistake for the true riches. While we are vainly saying, "We are rich and increased with goods," God has written that we are "wretched, and miserable, and poor, and blind, and naked" (Revelation 3:17).

Wealth and prosperity may be the costly spices and splendid decoration which embalm and entomb our spirituality. True strength lies in the godliness of the people. The personal holiness of the members of each church is the only true measure of strength. Any other test offends God, dishonors Christ, grieves the Holy Spirit, and degrades religion.

A church can often make the best showing of material strength when death in its deadliest form is feeding on its vital organs. There is hardly a more damaging delusion than to judge the conditions of a church by its material prosperity or church-related activity. Spiritual barrenness and rottenness in a church are generally hidden by a pleasant exterior and unusual growth. However, a spiritual church converts people from sin soundly, clearly, and fully. Then it puts them on the road to holiness where they strive to walk in a way that is pleasing to God.

This spirituality is not to be kept in a corner of the Church, but it is to be its primary and only business. God's Church must continue to do this work of converting sinners and perfecting saints in holiness. Whenever this work becomes secondary, or other interests are held to be its equivalent, then the Church becomes worldly. When material interests are emphasized, they come into prominence. Then the world comes to the throne and sways the scepter of Satan.

There is no surer way to make the Church worldly than to put its material prosperity in the forefront. This is the surest way to put Satan in charge. It is easy for material assessments to become priority by emphasizing them until the opinion is created that these are most important. When collecting money, building churches, and counting attendance becomes the evidence of church prosperity, then the world has a strong foothold, and Satan has achieved his purpose.

### Creating A Human Institution

Another scheme of Satan is to eliminate from the Church all the humble, self-denying ordinances which are offensive to unsanctified tastes and unregenerate hearts. He seeks to reduce the Church to a mere human institution—popular, natural, fleshly, and pleasing.

Satan has no scheme which can more thoroughly thwart God's high and holy purposes than to transform His Church into a human institution according to man's views. God's right arm is thereby paralyzed, the body of Christ becomes the body of Satan, light is turned into darkness and life into death.

Men who have religious positions are often blinded by a false attachment to what they think is truth and what they consider to honor Christ. They are found trying to eliminate from the teaching of Christ those painful, offensive, unpopular, and self-denying features to which the gospel owes all its saving beauty and power and which stamp it as divine.

From the life of Peter we have a painful and most instructive warning. "From that time forth began Jesus to shew unto His disciples, how that He must go unto Jerusalem, and suffer many things of the elders and chief priests and scribes, and be killed, and be raised again the third day. Then Peter took Him, began to rebuke Him, saying, Be it far from Thee, Lord: this shall not be unto Thee. But He turned, and said unto Peter, Get thee behind Me, Satan: thou art an offense unto Me; for thou savourest not the things that be of God, but those that be of men. Then said Jesus unto His disciples, If any man will come after Me, let him deny himself, and take up his cross, and follow

Me. For whosoever will save his life shall lose it: and whosoever will lose his life for My sake shall find it. For what is a man profited, if he shall gain the whole world, and lose his own soul? or what shall a man give in exchange for his soul? For the Son of Man shall come in the glory of His Father with His angels; and then He shall reward every man according to his works'' (Matthew 16:21-27).

Here is a lesson for all times and for all people. An apostle has become the mouthpiece of Satan! What an alarming, horrible, and revolting picture! An apostle, zealous for his Master's glory, advocating with fire and force a scheme which would forever destroy that glory! The apostle Peter became Satan's agent!

He is the same apostle who had just made that inspired confession, ''Thou art the Christ, the Son of the living God'' (Matthew 16:16), which placed him in highest honor with Christ and the Church! Before the words of that divine and marvelous confession died from his lips, this same apostle became the advocate of plans which would nullify his confession and destroy the eternal foundations of the Church.

### The Easy Way

Peter, a chief apostle, was advocating shemes which would discrown Christ of His Messiahship and bring heaven's favorite plan to a disastrous and shameful end! What destructive impulse compelled Peter? Satan entered him and, for the time being, achieved his purposes. But Christ reproves

Peter and in the reproof strikes a crushing blow at Satan.

"Get thee behind Me, Satan," is a reminder and duplicate of the wilderness temptation. "Thou art an offense (a stumbling block) to Me." This is the devil's trigger to catch Christ in the devil's trap—"Thou savourest not the things which be of God, but those that be of men" (verse 23). The devil is not in sight. Man appears and Satan's views are pressed to the front.

The things which men savor in church planning and church life are against God's plan. The high and holy principles of self-denial, of godly living, and of self-surrender to Christ are all against men's view of Christianity. The devil seeks to destroy the Church indirectly. Men's views eliminate all the unpopular principles of the cross—self-denial, life surrender, and separation from the world. When this is done, the devil runs the Church. Then the Church becomes popular, self-satisfying, modern, and progressive. But it is the devil's church, founded on principles pleasing in every way to flesh and blood.

Christ is no longer in the Church. There is no crucifixion of self, no crucifixion of the world, no second coming of Christ, no eternal judgment, no everlasting hell, no eternal heaven. Nothing is left that reminds us of God, because everything reeks of man. Man makes it the devil's church by turning Christ's Church over to human leaders. The world is sought and gained in the devil's church, but the soul and heaven are all lost to eternity.

The very heart of this disgraceful apostasy, this dethroning of Christ and enthroning of the devil, is to remove the Holy Spirit from His leadership in the Church. Satan's plan is to put unspiritual men in leadership to direct the Church. Men of great ability and men with the powers of leadership have often displaced God's leadership. The ambition for leadership and the enthronement of human leaders is the doom and seal of apostasy. There is no leadership in God's Church except the leadership of the Holy Spirit. The man who has the most of God's Spirit is God's chosen leader. He is zealous for the Spirit's sovereignty, ambitious to be the least, the slave of all.

# Chapter Six

# SATAN'S SUBVERSION OF THE CHURCH

*"Jesus answered, Verily, verily, I say unto thee, Except a man be born of water and of the Spirit, he cannot enter the Kingdom of God. That which is born of the flesh is flesh; and that which is born of the Spirit is spirit. Marvel not that I said unto thee, Ye must be born again"*—John 3:5-7.

*"Ye worship ye know not what. . . .But the hour cometh, and now is, when the true worshippers shall worship the Father in spirit and in truth: for the Father seeketh such to worship him. God is a Spirit: and they that worship him must worship him in spirit and in truth"*—John 4:22a,23,24.

There are two ways of directing the Church: God's way and the devil's way. God's way and man's way of running the Church are entirely opposite. Man's wise plans, thoughtful resources, and easy solutions are Satan's devices. The cross is retired and the world comes in. Self-denial is eliminated, and all seems bright, cheerful, and prosperous. Satan's hand is on the controls, and men's schemes prevail. The Church fails under these devices of men, and the bankruptcy is so complete that the court of heaven will not even appoint a successor for the collapsed corporation.

All of God's plans have the mark of the cross on them, and all His plans have death to self in them. All God's plans have crucifixion to the world in them. But men's plans ignore the offense of the cross or despise it. Men's plans have no profound, stern, or sacrificial denial in them. Their gain is of the world. How many of these destructive elements does the devil bring into the Church, until all the holy aims and heavenly purposes of the Church are retired and forgotten?

## Society Versus Salvation

One of these Satanic devices is to pervert the aims of the Church. He deludes church leaders into thinking that the main purpose of the Church today is not so much to save individuals out of society, as to save society; not to save souls so much as to save the bodies of men; not to save men out of a community so much as to save men and manhood in the community. The world, not the individual, is the subject of redemption.

This popular, seductive, and deadly fallacy entirely subverts the very foundation of Christ's Church. This trend is so strong that it will sweep away every vestige of the spiritual and eternal. For this reason, we must watch, work, and speak with sleepless vigilance, tireless energy, and fearless boldness. The attitude and open declaration of much of the religious teaching we now hear is in the same strain and spirit which characterized the Unitarian, Jewish, and rationalistic thinking of a century ago.

To save society is a kind of religious fad to which much enterprising church work is committed. Advanced thinkers have elaborated the same idea. They do not realize their true condition, which is one of going backward and not going forward. This backward step entombs religion in the grave where Judaism has been buried all these centuries. It may well be in agreement with the idle dreams of the worldly rabbis to think of regenerating the world and ignoring the individual.

The phrase "to save the world" has a pompous sound. It seems right for the Church to apply itself to bettering the temporal surroundings of the individual and improving his sanitary conditions; to lessen the bad smells that greet his nose; to diminish the bacteria in his water; and to put granite in the pavement for him to walk on instead of wood or brick. All this sounds fine and agrees well with a material age. It becomes practical in operation and provides obvious, imposing results. But does this agree with the sublime dignity and essential aim of the Church?

Do we need the Church to accomplish these purposes? Concerned councilmen, an efficient street commissioner, and the ordinary vigilance of the average policeman will secure these results in the best way. They need no Church, no Bible, no Christ, no personal holiness to accomplish these purposes. If the Church concentrates its efforts on results which can be better accomplished by other agencies, the Church will soon be regarded as a nuisance and lose its influence in the world.

## A Unique Institution

The purpose of the Church of God is far superior to these childish dreams and fruitless philosophies. Its purpose is to regenerate and sanctify the individual, to prepare him by purifying and training for the high pursuits of eternal life.

The Church is like the net cast into the sea. The purpose is not to change the sea but to catch the fishes out of the sea. Let the sea roll on its essential nature while the net catches its fishes. What if fishermen spent all their energies trying by some chemical process to change the essential elements of the sea, vainly hoping to improve the stock of fish? They would never catch any fish! If the Church used this method, personal holiness would be impossible, and heaven would be stricken from our creed, life, and hope.

To save the world and ignore the individual is not only utopian but destructive in every way. To save the world is a commendable goal, but it will result in making the Church worldly and unfit for her holy and sublime mission. Christ said that gaining the world and saving the man are opposing objectives. Christ teaches Peter that his Satanic devices would gain the world to and for the

Church, but would lose the soul. Everything would seem to contribute to the cause when in reality all was death.

The Church is distinctly, preeminently, and absolutely a spiritual institution. It is an institution created, vitalized, possessed, and directed by the Spirit of God. Her ministers and doctrines have appeal, relevance, and power only when they are channels of the Holy Spirit. It is His indwelling and inspiration which give the Church its divine character and accomplish its divine purposes.

## The Spiritual Subversion

If the devil can by any methods shut the Holy Spirit out of the Church, he has effectively prevented the Church from being God's Church on earth. He accomplishes this by retiring from the Church the agencies or agents which the Holy Spirit uses. Satan displaces them with natural devices which are rarely if ever the channels used by the Holy Spirit. Christ announced this unchangeable, universal law when He said, "That which is born of the flesh is flesh; that which is born of the Spirit is spirit" (John 3:6).

A church may have a holy preacher, a man of great prayerfulness, of great grace, filled with the Spirit. Satan will use any method to retire him and put in a man who does not pray, but who is eloquent and popular. The church may seem to have gained, but it has gained by the substitution of natural for spiritual forces, a gain which has unknowingly revolutionized the Church.

A church can be led by holy men who are not highly cultured, but well-versed in the deep things of God; who are strong in devotion to Christ and His cause, but not wealthy or of high social position. A church may change these officers and put in men who are in every way decent and moral but who are not noted for prayer and piety. If you put in men of high social position who are capable administrators, the church scarcely notices the change except for the marked improvement in finances. But an invisible and powerful change has taken place in the church. It has changed from a spiritual church to a worldly one. The change from noonday to midnight is not more extreme than that.

At this point, Satan is doing his deadliest and most damning work. It is more deadly and damning because it is unnoticed, unseen, producing no shock, and exciting no alarm.

It is not by the obvious works of evil that Satan perverts the Church, but by quiet displacement and unnoticed substitution. The higher is being retired, the spiritual gives place to the social, and the divine is eliminated because it is made secondary.

The perversion and subversion of the Church is achieved by Satan when the spiritual forces are retired or made subordinate to the natural; when social entertainment, and not edification, becomes the desired goal. This process is intended to soften and modify the distinctly spiritual aims of the Church and to broaden what is called the rigid exclusiveness of spiritual narrowness.

But in the end it eliminates all that is distinctly spiritual. That which is in any sense deeply religious will not survive the death of the spiritual. The leaders lose sight of spiritual edification as the purpose of God's Church. Instead, entertainment that is pleasing and pleasant comes to the front. The social forces not only retire the spiritual forces, but effectually destroy them.

### The Modern Church

A modern church with its kitchen and parlor, with its club and gymnasium, and with its ministries to the flesh and to the world is both suggestive and alarming. What a contrast there is between the principles which the early Church originated and fostered and those which the modern and progressive Church presents as substitutes.

The original churches were faithfully spiritual. Their only purpose was to strengthen and cultivate all the elements which combine to make a deep and clear experience of God. They were training schools for spiritual life. They never lingered in the regions of the moral, the aesthetic, and the mental. They fostered no desires or inclinations which were not spiritual and did not minister to the soul's progress.

The early Church took it for granted that all who came to them really desired to flee from the wrath to come and were sincerely yearning after full redemption. They considered it their obligation to furnish these seekers with the most sacred and exacting assistance. It never occurred to them that entertainment and social gatherings were channels through which God's grace would flow and foster spiritual growth.

These social and fleshly forces are regarded in many denominations as the perfection of spiritual things. These events are arrayed as the mature fruit of spiritual piety, flavored and perfected by its culture and progress. They are ordained as the handmaidens of the prayer and testimony meeting. We object most seriously to the union of the worldly and the spiritual. What have they in common? "Can two walk together, except they be agreed?" (Amos 3:3).

What elements of piety are fostered by entertainment and social gatherings? What phases of spiritual life do they promote? What feature of the gymnasium produces faith? Where do you find any elements which are aids to piety? How do social parties produce a more prayerful and holy life? How does it bring the soul nearer to God? How does it form or strengthen the ties of Christian fellowship? Are social clubs not frivolous and worldly? Do parties not cater to and suit the tastes of the carnal and worldly? What unity of purpose and spirit is there between worldly entertainment and witnessing for Christ? The one is intensely spiritual. The other has in it no evidence of spiritual benefit.

We might as well add to the list of heavenly helpers, the skating rink, calisthenics, and the gymnasium. If the young people desire to join a club, enjoy a social gathering, or play parlor games let them do so. But do not deceive them and degrade holiness by calling these things holy institutions that feed the spiritual life.

## Creating A Revolution

Disguise it as we may; reason about it as we will; apologize for it as we do; the truth is, we have lost that intensity of our personal spiritual experience. We have lost that deep conviction about eternal things which are evident features of all great spiritual movements.

Many preachers and people have fallen so low in their experience that they do not cherish these distinct and strongly spiritual methods. Instead, they are devising plans and organizations to gratify their non-spiritual desires which are midway between Christ and the world. While these desires are not essentially wrong, they do not possess one grain of spiritual power and can never be the channels of heavenly communication.

It is said we cannot get church people to attend distinctly spiritual meetings. What is the problem? Are the institutions worn out and no longer of value to the humble, pious soul? Who will dare affirm this? They say the desires of the people are low and perverted. Should we then change the methods to suit unsanctified appetites? No, instead let us tone up their appetites for spiritual things and elevate the tastes of our people.

Let the revolution begin with the preacher. Let

him wrestle with God until his ordination vow becomes revitalized so that everyone can feel the pressure of his goal, the intensity of his zeal, the singleness of his purpose, and the holiness of his life. Let the people catch the fire and purpose of his heart until all press on to the regions of perfect love, panting for all the fullness of God. Under this united, divine inspiration, worldly entertainment will be forgotten and become stale. Then, the spiritual meetings of the church will become attractive and delightful.

The Church cannot become allied with non-spiritual agencies. By doing this she breaks the tension of her faith and discards the Holy Spirit. She cannot be the supplier of unsanctified desires. Neither is it her business to fall down to the beggarly task of entertaining the people. This is her saddest mistake: when her evening services are surrendered to concerts and lectures; her praise turned into worldly music; her classrooms into parlors; and her social gatherings more popular than her prayer meetings. Then the house of God becomes a house of feasting instead of a house of prayer. The unity of the Spirit and the holy brotherhood are displaced and destroyed to make room for social affinities and worldly attractions.

It is the Church's high and royal duty to maintain her spotless fidelity to her Lord, to stress holiness, and use every means for its advancement and perfection. When this is done, spiritual character and holiness will order all the rest.

# Chapter Seven

# OVERCOMING THE ENEMY OF GOD

*"I have written unto you, young men, because you are strong, and the word of God abideth in you, and ye have overcome the wicked one. Love not the world. If any man love the world, the love of the Father is not in him. For all that is in the world, the lust of the flesh, and the lust of the eyes, and the pride of life, is not of the Father, but of the world. And the world passeth away, and the lust thereof: but he that doeth the will of God abideth for ever"*—1 John 2:14-17.

The world should be renounced by every true disciple of Christ. To love the world and the things of the world puts us in open enmity to God. If we have a relationship of love or friendship to the world, we are the enemies of God. We need commit no other sin except that of having an attachment to the world. By that alone, we are the enemies of God.

Christ Jesus said that between the world and His disciples there would be hatred. Discipleship to both Himself and to the world is impossible. The call, the touch, and choice of Christ when accepted and obeyed becomes the secret and the source of the world's hatred.

Jesus declares the inevitable enmity of the world to His followers: "The world hath hated them, because they are not of the world, even as I am not of the world" (John 17:14). Again, in the priestly prayer, He declares this distinct and eternal separation and conflict: "They are not of the world, even as I am not of the world." By virtue of their relationship to Christ, they are separated from and are in conflict with the world.

## Who Is An Adulterer?

The two persons, Jesus and Adam, their natures, affinities, and opposition are declared in the clearest language: "The first man is of the earth, earthy: the second man is the Lord from heaven. As is the earthy, such are they also that are earthy: and as is the heavenly, such are they also that are heavenly. And as we have borne the image of the earthly, we shall also bear the image of the heavenly" (1 Corinthians 15:47-49).

Opposition to the world is strongly declared and demanded. The love of the world is hostile to and destructive of the love of God. The two cannot coexist.

"Ye adulterers and adulteresses, know ye not that the friendship of the world is enmity with God? Whosoever therefore will be a friend of the world is the enemy of God" (James 4:4).

Nothing is more explicit than this, nothing is

more commanding, authoritative, and more exacting. "Love not the world" (1 John 2:15). Nothing is more offensive to God, nothing is more criminal, more abominable. Loving the world violates the most sacred relationship of the soul with God. "Adulterers"—purity departs, while shame and illicit intercourse exist. Friendship with the world is heaven's greatest crime and God's greatest enemy.

The world is one of the enemies which must be fought and conquered on the way to heaven. "For this is the love of God, that we keep His commandments: and His commandments are not grievous. For whatsoever is born of God overcometh the world: and this is the victory that overcometh the world, even our faith. Who is he that overcometh the world, but he that believeth that Jesus is the Son of God?" (1 John 5:3-5).

The gospel is represented as a training school in which denying worldly desires is one part of its curriculum. "For the grace of God that bringeth salvation hath appeared to all men, teaching us that, denying ungodliness and worldly lusts, we should live soberly, righteously and godly, in this present world; looking for that blessed hope, and the glorious appearing of the great God and our Saviour Jesus Christ; who gave Himself for us, that He might redeem us from all iniquity, and purify unto Himself a peculiar people, zealous of good works" (Titus 2:11-14).

There is something in the world which makes it a deadly enemy to the salvation of Christ and which poisons us against heaven.

## What Is The World?

What is "this world" which so effectually alien-
ates us from heaven and puts us in flagrant enmity
to God? Why is it that our friendship with the
world violates our wedding vow to God? Why is it
that love of the world is enmity to God and criminal to the most abominable degree?

What is it? "The world, the lust of the flesh, and
the lust of the eyes, and the pride of life" (1 John
2:16). What are they?

*The world* includes the mass of humanity that is
alienated from God and therefore hostile to the
cause of Christ. It involves worldly affairs, earthly
things, riches, pleasures, and pursuits which are
shallow, frail, and fleeting. They stir desire, draw
away from God, and are obstacles to the cause of
Christ. The divorced or torn relationship between
heaven and earth, between God and His creatures,
finds its expression in the term "the world."

Our English word *desire* expresses the meaning
of the word *lust*. It includes the world of active
lusts and desires which controls the seat of desire
and the natural appetites.

Alford's Commentary says: "The world was con-
stituted at first in Adam, well pleasing to God and
obedient to Him. It was man's world, and in man it
was summed up. In man the world fell into the
darkness of selfish pursuits. Man became material-
ized in spirit and dragged down so as to become
worldly and sensual. The world is a man's world in

his fall from God. The *lust of the flesh* is human nature in opposition to God. The *lust of the eyes* is that sense which takes note of physical things and is inflamed by them. The *pride of life* is the manner of worldly men whereby pride is displayed and pomp is cherished."

Bengel says: *"The lust of the flesh* means those things on which the sense of enjoyment, taste, and touch are fed. The *lusts of the eyes* means those things by which the senses of investigation—the eye and sight, hearing, smelling, and feeling—are occupied. *Pride of life* means when anyone assumes too much about himself in words or actions. Even those who do not love arrogance of life may possibly pursue the *lust of the eyes*. Even those who have overpowered this fault still frequently retain the *lust of the flesh*. This problem prevails among the poor, the middle class, and the powerful. It is even found among those who appear to exercise self-denial."

John Wesley says: "The 'desire of the flesh' means the pleasures of the outward senses, whether of taste, smell, or touch. The 'desire of the eye' refers to the pleasures of the imagination to which the eye is chiefly subservient. It is that internal sense whereby we long for the grand, the new, or the beautiful. The 'pride of life' means everything that we use to generate respect from other people—fancy clothing, houses, furniture, and manners of living—anything which gratifies our pride and vanity. It therefore directly includes the desire for praise and involves a certain degree of covetousness. All these desires are not from God, but from the prince of this world.''

## The Enemy Of Heaven

This world arrays itself and all its forces against heaven. Worldliness is the epidemic foe to heaven. To live for this world is to lose heaven because of an opposite attraction. The Son of God declares of His disciples and reiterates to His Father: ''Thou gavest (them) Me out of the world'' (John 17:6,16). It remains true to this hour that all the true disciples of Jesus are not of the world, but are chosen out of the world, have renounced the world, and are crucified to the world.

What gives the world its fatal charms? What makes its charms so deadly? Sometimes its beauty is all withered, its brightness all night, its hope all despair, its joy the bitterest anguish, and all its prospects decay and desert. But still it holds and binds. We hate to leave it. What is the source of its deadly sorcery and its fatal snares? What is the source of its malignant hate, its hostility to God, and its alienation from heaven?

This world is the devil's world. In that fatal hour when man fell from his allegiance and devotion to God, he carried the world with him in his rebellion against God. Man was the world's ruler and the world fell with its master. This is the reason for its vicious rivalry and its intense opposition to heaven. The devil has his kingdom here. It is his princedom. He clothes it with all beauty and seductive power as the rival of heaven.

Heaven's trinity of foes are the world, the flesh, and the devil. The world is first, the most powerful and engaging. All three center in evil because the devil inspires and inflames them. The flesh wars against the spirit simply because the devil inflames its desires. The world gets its deadly and fascinating snares from the devil. The world is not simply the ally, but it is the instrument and the agent of Satan. It represents him with the most servile and complete loyalty.

## How To Overcome The World

The text from First John already quoted, "Love not the world, neither the things that are in the world," needs, for its full understanding, to have the preface which reads: "I write unto you, young men, because ye have overcome the wicked one. I write unto you, little children, because ye have known the Father. I have written unto you, fathers, because ye have known him that is from the beginning. I have written unto you, young men, because ye are strong, and the word of God abideth in you, and ye have overcome the wicked one" (1 John 2:13,14).

In order to "overcome the wicked one," the world, its love, and its things must be renounced. At the threshold of many church doors are written these words which belong to every soul's true betrothal to Christ: "Dost thou renounce the devil and all his works, the vain pomp and glory of the world, with all covetous desires of the same, and the carnal desires of the flesh, so that thou wilt not follow or be led by them?"

"I renounce them all," was the answer solemnly given and the preacher, the people, and our own hearts said, "Amen." And amen let it be now and forever.

This world must be renounced and this means to renounce Satan. This is the deadliest blow to his rule. The friendship with the world violates our marriage vows to heaven.

James, in his severe denunciations of the world, makes friendship with the world criminal. He declares that to be the friend of the world is to be the enemy of God. We cannot understand this unless we realize he is declaring that the world's friendship is the devil's religion, earthly, sensual, and devilish. We can get back to God only by renouncing the friendship with the world and by cleansing our hearts and hands of its soiling touch. We draw near to God by resisting the devil. We resist the devil by renouncing the world.

## Counterfeit Religion

The apostle James sums up the distinct characteristics of the devil's world-counterfeit religion. Passion, appetite, and pleasure reign and make war (James 4:1-3). How much of this passion, pleasure, and world religion has there been in the Church? Too often its history is a history of passion, strife, ambition, and blood. Its ecumenical councils are the battlefield of passion in its unbridled, most destructive form. Earthly, sensual, and devilish is the divine stigma which marks and mars ecclesiastical history.

Many modern church members and churchgoers are friends of the world, its advocates and lovers. They only say prayers in order not to miss praying. There is no drawing near to God, no fighting against the devil and driving him from the field of action. Their religion, its ceremonies, and its worship descend not from above, but are earthly, natural, and devilish.

"Submit to God" and "resist the devil" is the keynote of unworldly religion. A personal God and a personal devil are among the primary articles of creed and experience in true religion. Surrender to God, draw near to Him, and live close to Him. Fight against the devil and get rid of him by denouncing and rejecting the world.

Chapter Eight

# MOBILIZING THE WORLD'S FORCES

*"And you hath he quickened, who were dead in trespasses and sins; wherein in time past ye walked according to the course of this world, according to the prince of the power of the air, the spirit that now worketh in the children of disobedience: Among whom also we all had our conversation in times past in the lusts of the flesh, fulfilling the desires of the flesh and of the mind; and were by nature the children of wrath, even as others"*—Ephesians 2:1-3.

The divine warning against the course of the world, against the fashion of the world, and against the spirit of the world is given because the devil is directing the world's course. The devil is creating the world's spirit, and the devil is cutting the pattern of the world's fashion.

The touch of the world pollutes because Satan's fingers are in its touch. Its desires are deadly and heaven-quenching because Satan kindles its desires. The world and its things are contraband in Christian warfare because Satan is the ruler of the world and the administrator of its affairs.

In Ephesians, Satan and his legions are called the world rulers: "Put on the whole armour of God, that ye may be able to stand against the wiles of the devil. For we wrestle not against flesh and blood, but against principalities, against powers, against the rulers of the darkness of this world, against spiritual wickedness in high places" (Ephesians 6:11,12).

The world rulers are principalities and powers under the direction of the devil. They rule this world by ruling the things which rule this world!

## The Forces Of This World

Satan seizes and directs all the mighty forces of this world! *War* is seized by Satan, and it is no longer the patriot's struggle for freedom or the defense of home and native land. Instead, it becomes the tool of despotism, crushes liberty, and enslaves freedom. War carries on a campaign of lust, rape, cruelty, desolation, and death.

*Money* is another of the world's ruling forces which could be used to beautify the earth and to lay up a good foundation against the time to come. It should be used to ease the burdens of the poor, to banish poverty, and to brighten the homes of widows and orphans. Money is a mighty world-ruling power. The devil rules it, and, instead of flowing at the command of compassionate love, it is diverted by Satan for selfish and unholy purposes. Satan excites men to covetousness and hardens them into callousness. Men become illustrious and esteemed when they are money-getters and money-keepers.

*Education* is another mighty world-ruling force. Satan chains it, and it becomes the source of pride and ungodly power. Its mighty engineering is turned into "higher criticism." Under the guise of Christian learning, education becomes the most powerful ally to Satan by unsettling faith in God's Word and opening a wide door of skepticism in the temple of God.

In Ephesians the devil is called the "prince of the power of the air." The *natural forces* of the world are under his dangerous control. How many destructive storms and cyclones is he responsible for?

## The Flesh And The Mind

"And you hath he quickened, who were dead in trespasses and sins; wherein in time past ye walked according to the course of this world, according to the prince of the power of the air, the spirit that now worketh in the children of disobedience. Among whom also we all had our conversation in times past in the lusts of our flesh, fulfilling the desires of the flesh and of the mind; and were by nature the children of wrath, even as others" (Ephesians 2:1-3).

Paul speaks of himself and the saints. They formerly lived in Satan's kingdom, and he ruled them by the lusts of the flesh—"fulfilled the desires of the flesh and the mind."

In these verses we see how Satan rules throughout the world. He is the god of this world, and he excites its desires, both low and high—low in *the desires of the flesh* and high in *the desires of the mind*. The world fills the passions and chains the mind in its high worldly pursuits and refined tastes. Yet, it is all of Satan. The "lust of the flesh, the lust of the eyes and pride of life," these are of the world and Satan is the exciter of them: "Then when lust hath conceived, it bringeth forth sin. . .and death" (James 1:15).

"We know that whosoever is begotten of God sinneth not; but he that is begotten of God keepeth himself, and that wicked one toucheth him not. And we know that we are of God, and the whole world lieth in wickedness (in the evil one)" (1 John 5:18,19). The world "lieth" means that it is in the power of the devil, is held in subjection by him, and is fixed and established. The devil is pictured as trying to kindle into a flame the desires which may remain in a good man's heart after conversion. He also enfolds in his arms the whole world and makes it subject to his power and submissive to his absolute control.

### The Devil's Heaven

When the world comes in, it comes in many forms. At whatever door and in whatever form it comes, the world is always the devil's servant. It comes in to do his work as his most obedient and faithful slave. When the world comes in, dressed in its most seductive and beautiful garb, the devil has fashioned its clothing and ordered its coming.

The world is the devil's heaven. Its rest, crown, and reward are here. When the world comes in, God's heaven goes out. It fades from the eye and heart. The struggle for it ends, and God's heaven, with its fadeless and eternal glories, is lost.

In these statements from the Bible about the world and the devil, we see why the world opposes heaven. We realize the enmity between the two. Heaven is Christ's place, the place where He is, and to which He wants men to come. The world is Satan's place. His power is here. To fix our hearts on the world is to be loyal to him. To fix our hearts on heaven is to be loyal to Christ.

Here we have the reason for the cruel hatred of the world for Jesus and why it has so bitterly persecuted His followers. We see why the Spirit lusteth against the flesh and the flesh against the Spirit. We see why these are not only contrary to one another, but at war with one another. The devil is in the flesh and rules it. Christ is in the Spirit. This world leads away from Christ. It is the invincible foe of Christ.

This great truth is illustrated and enforced by the fact that Christ's work is to get possession of the world and make its power accomplish His purposes. But He establishes a Kingdom of heaven which is not of this world. A new power has come in, a new Kingdom established, and a new world made. It will take the fires of the judgment and the new creative power to make a new heaven and a new earth. The stains and ruin of the devil's death-dealing hands must be removed and this corrupted, yet beautiful, world prepared for God's holy purposes.

The Christian is called to renounce his allegiance to the world. By his very relationship to Jesus Christ, he is lifted out of the world's deadly embraces, and its polluting charms are broken. In this subserviency of the world to the devil, we have the reason for the world's intense hatred of Jesus Christ. We can see why the world has armed itself with all its forces under the power of the devil to destroy the cause of Christ. The world's opposition and enmity have always been against true religion, but often its smiles are more fatal than its hate.

Chapter Nine

# HOW POWERFUL IS THE DEVIL?

*"Now there was a day when the sons of God came to present themselves before the Lord, and Satan came also with them. And the Lord said unto Satan, Whence comest thou? Then Satan answered the Lord, and said, From going to and fro in the earth, and from walking up and down in it. And the Lord said unto Satan, Hast thou considered my servant Job, that there is none like him in the earth, a perfect and an upright man, one that feareth God, and escheweth evil? Then Satan answered the Lord, and said, Doth Job fear God for nought? Hast not thou made an hedge about him, and about his house, and about all that he hath on every side? thou hast blessed the work of his hands, and his substance is increased in the land. But put forth thine hand now, and touch all that he hath, and he will curse thee to thy face. And the Lord said unto Satan, Behold, all that he hath is in thy power; only upon himself put not forth thine hand. So Satan went forth from the presence of the*

*Lord"*—Job 1:6-12.

In all we have seen, instead of minimizing the power of the devil, Jesus exalts him to the pinnacle of power as the prince of this world.

In the significant events of Christ's life, the devil is the one evil agent which Christ has in mind and to whose rule He is opposed. We have seen how soon the devil followed in the wake of our Lord's baptism at the Jordan. Satan came to Jesus after He was anointed of the Holy Spirit and entered into His public ministry.

When He first commissioned His disciples, one of their assignments was to "cast out devils." When the seventy returned to report their work to Christ, they said, with evident surprise and gratification, "Even the devils are subject unto us through Thy name." He replied: "I beheld Satan as lightning fall from heaven" (Luke 10:17,18). When He is opening their hearts to receive the great Comforter, He declares that the Holy Spirit was "to reprove the world. . .of judgment, because the prince of this world is judged" (John 16:8,11).

In one of His impassioned outbreaks, as the pain of His great agony draws nearer, Jesus cries, "Now is my soul troubled" (John 12:27). The darkness is relieved by a gleam of light in which He sees the ruin of Satan's kingdom and the devil spoiled, dethroned, and cast out by the power of His cross: "Now is the judgment of this world: now shall the prince of this world be cast out. And I, if I be lifted up from the earth, will draw all men unto Me" (John 12:31).

But as the darkness grows deeper and the anguish more bitter, He sees the approaching form of him who controls the powers of darkness. Hushed into silence in the presence of this relentless and cruel foe, the Son of God says to His sorrowing and awe-struck disciples: "Hereafter I will not talk much with you: for the prince of this world cometh, and hath nothing in Me" (John 14:30).

## Satan's Power Over Men

The devil's sad and mighty influence is further seen within the circle of the chosen disciples. Peter staggers under the blow of the devil. The shameful denial by Peter is referred to by Christ: "Simon, Simon, behold Satan hath desired to have you, that he might sift you as wheat: but I have prayed for thee, that thy faith fail not; and, when thou art converted, strengthen thy brethren" (Luke 22:31,32).

Jesus Christ acknowledges the great power and authority which the devil has in the present deranged order of things. He declares, "Now is the judgment of this world: now shall the prince of this world be cast out" (John 12:31).

How defiant Satan is! He opposes Christ stubbornly with reckless and often successful courage. Into the chosen circle of the twelve he entered, into the one who had been trusted as their treasurer, the receiver, and the disburser of their money and their charity.

One of the sacred twelve was possessed and moved to carry out in the most hypocritical, false way Satan's infamous designs. He came very close to adding Peter to the black list of his disgraceful recruits. It is evident that the devil had much to do with Peter's dastardly denial, his lying and blasphemy. The words of Christ make this plain, "And the Lord said unto Simon, Simon, behold Satan hath desired to have you, that he may sift you as wheat: But I have prayed for thee, that thy faith fail not; and when thou art converted, strengthen thy brethren. And he said unto Him, Lord, I am ready to go with Thee, both unto prison, and to death. And He said, I tell thee, Peter, the cock shall not crow this day, before that thou shalt thrice deny that thou knowest Me" (Luke 22:31-34).

In the parable of the sower, Christ sets forth the unseen but powerful influence which the devil exerts to neutralize the Word of God. In the record of this parable by Matthew, the devil is termed the "wicked one." This is a statement of his personality and of the concentration of his pre-eminent wickedness. He snatches away the seed of the Word with vigilant and diabolical hate. "Then cometh the devil, and taketh away the word" (Luke 8:12). He is the destroyer of the seeds of good. Satan is so powerful that the incorruptible and eternal Word of God is prevented from accomplishing its saving efforts because of his vigilance and influence over the mind.

## Power To Afflict

In the story of Job and his trials, we see the Sabeans and Chaldeans ready to respond to Satan's suggestion to make their raids on Job's herds. Satan's power is not limited to outside influence, but it is direct and powerful, getting on the inside. His suggestions of evil are almost godlike sometimes. They excite our passions or principles so we cannot see the wrong until it is too late. This was true in the case of Satan's suggestion to David to number Israel.

His power is so great that even the best men, who are able to resist his temptations, for a time come under his power. The Christians at Smyrna were so under his power that, while he could not alienate their affections or disturb their loyalty, he could put them in prison. Paul felt all his life the buffeting inflicted by Satan's power.

Peter was in Satan's hands and was on the verge of giving in to his power. Job was for a while put under his power. He was driven and afflicted as if in a cruel tempest in which everything was wrecked and lost except his patience. How great was Satan's power to destroy fortune, family, friends, and reputation!

The Son of God was led to the temple by the fearful spell of Satan. Angels retired, heaven hushed its music, and all was draped in silence. All creation trembled in awe while Satan's dread power was allowed to expend its dark forces on heaven's Anointed One.

The power of disease was also in the devil's hands. He smote Job. Christ said of the woman with the spirit of infirmity: "Ought not this woman, being a daughter of Abraham, whom Satan hath bound, lo, these eighteen years, be loosed from this bond on the sabbath day?" (Luke 13:16).

Doubtless much sickness is due to the power of the devil. To this there is reference in the statements of Christ's work. "When the even was come, they brought unto Him many that were possessed with devils: and He cast out the spirits with His word, and healed all that were sick: That it might be fulfilled which was spoken by Isaiah the prophet, saying, Himself took our infirmities, and bare our sicknesses" (Matthew 8:16,17). "How God anointed Jesus of Nazareth with the Holy Ghost and with power; who went about doing good, and healing all that were oppressed of the devil; for God was with Him" (Acts 10:38).

## Power Over The Body

Satan's power did not extend to death in Job's case, but he did destroy the lives of his children. Satan was able to hold the Smyrna Christians in prison only ten days, but thousands of others he held unto death. His own cruel, deadly hands weaved for them the martyr's crown of gold and glory.

The power of the devil over the body is further seen and illustrated by a number of cases of demonic possessions in the New Testament. The devil had possession of the bodies of some people,

80

using his demons to control them. Some of the cases were fearfully tormented in body and almost wrecked in mind. Others had functions of the body suspended: some were made dumb by him; others were made deaf; and still others were made blind. These cases were many in number and of great variety. Among the most distressing cases were those who were not great sinners. Instead, the young, comparatively innocent ones were the victims of Satan's dread power. The whole person came under the power of this alien spirit. The power of Satan, his nearness and personality, had a constant and destructive manifestation in these cases.

It has been well said that the gospel narratives are distinctly pledged to the historic truth of these occurrences of demon possession. Either they are true or the gospels are false. They relate to us words spoken by the Lord Jesus in which the personality and presence of the devil are distinctly stated. Now either our Lord spoke these words or He did not. If He did not, then we must also set aside the concurrent testimony of the seventy disciples. In other words, we establish a principle which will overthrow every fact related in the gospels.

# Chapter Ten

## THE RULERS OF DARKNESS

*"And he shewed me Joshua the high priest standing before the angel of the Lord, and Satan standing at his right hand to resist him. And the Lord said unto Satan, the Lord rebuke thee, O Satan; even the Lord that hath chosen Jerusalem rebuke thee: is not this a brand plucked out of the fire? Now Joshua was clothed with filthy garments, and stood before the angel. And he answered and spake unto those that stood before him, saying, Take away the filthy garments from him. And unto him he said, Behold, I have caused thine iniquity to pass from thee, and I will clothe thee with change of raiment"*— Zechariah 3:1-4.

The power of Satan is far greater than that of God's highest and earthly saints. In the third chapter of Zechariah, we have the picture of his power with God's high official representatives. Joshua, the high priest, and the angel of the Lord are there. Standing at Joshua's right hand to resist all his righteous acts is Satan. Joshua and the angel realize their insufficiency when contending with Satan and send a cry to heaven, "The Lord rebuke thee."

Jude gives us this interesting statement: "Michael the archangel, when contending with the devil he disputed about the body of Moses, durst not bring him a railing accusation, but said, The Lord rebuke thee" (Jude 9).

This obscure text teaches us something regarding this contest between Michael and the devil. It clearly shows that an archangel's strength is not sufficient to contend single-handed and alone with the devil.

## The Power Of The Unseen

Daniel gives a side glance into the power and conflict which exist in the unseen and spiritual world which lie so near our own. This invisible world has much to do with how our spiritual battles are fought and victories won. Daniel had been praying three weeks before the angel and the answer came. "Then said he unto me, Fear not, Daniel: for from the first day that thou didst set thine heart to understand, and to chasten thyself before thy God, thy words were heard, and I am come for thy words. But the prince of the kingdom of Persia withstood me one and twenty days: but lo, Michael, one of the chief princes, came to help me" (Daniel 10:12,13).

We see how Satan works. If he cannot keep people from praying, he can cause delay in the answer to prayer. In this way he tries to discourage and break down our faith. He wants us to minimize the power of urgent, persistent praying.

Satan has power to cast into prison. To the little church at Smyrna, Jesus Christ writes in commendation, warning, and consolation: "Fear none of those things which thou shalt suffer: behold, the devil shall cast some of you into prison, that ye may be tried; and ye shall have tribulation ten days: be thou faithful unto death, and I will give thee a crown of life" (Revelation 2:10).

There are special seats or headquarters of his power, places where the devil makes his home and rules with an absolute control. Christ refers to this in His letter to the church of Pergamos: "I know thy works, and where thou dwellest, even where Satan's seat is: and thou holdest fast My name, and hast not denied My faith, even in those days wherein Antipas was My faithful martyr, who was slain among you, where Satan dwelleth" (Revelation 2:13).

Some said they were Jews, but they were called the "synagogue of Satan." Are there churches which are called Christian, but are churches of Satan? In Christ's letters to the seven churches in Asia, we see how the ascended and enthroned Son of God presents the same view of the devil. The "depths" of Satan are referred to in the address to Thyatira (Revelation 2:24). In this Revelation of Christ to John, the devil is still declared to be "the great dragon, the old serpent, the devil, and Satan" (20:2). He is declared to have great "wrath."

# Satanic Worship

The devil's power is greatly and strangely enhanced by his system of worship which, while it degrades, fascinates many people. The system of pagan worship and devotion is very powerful. It holds its devotees by iron chains. It is not a work of chance, and it does not spring from native religious instincts. It is a system of rare power and skill constructed by a graduate in the craft of seduction and delusion. Satan's hand is at the root of all pagan worship—planning, ordering, and inspiring it. It is this fact which gives it strength and influence.

Jeroboam perverted the religious instinct and debased worship for sinister, worldly, and selfish purposes. It is said he ordained priests for the devils. The psalmist declared they sacrificed unto devils.

The New Testament declares that "the things which the Gentiles sacrifice, they sacrifice to devils, and not to God: and I would not that ye should have fellowship with devils. Ye cannot drink the cup of the Lord, and the cup of devils: ye cannot be partakers of the Lord's table, and of the table of devils" (1 Corinthians 10:20,21). Again we have it declared, "Now the Spirit speaketh expressly, that in the latter times some shall depart from the faith, giving heed to seducing spirits, and doctrines of devils" (1 Timothy 4:1).

The intensity and power of the devil's worship is illustrated and enforced in the last book of the

New Testament. It shows how his worship will increase in intensity and war against the worship of the Lamb. Since almost the beginning of man, there have been rival altars and rival worship. The devil is the author, inspirer, and protector of the one; and Christ is the author, inspirer, and protector of true and pure worship. There are wonders and miracles in both. There are martyrs in the false and devilish, as well as in the true and heavenly.

## Satan's Rank And File

Revelation summarizes the situation: "And they had a king over them, which is the angel of the bottomless pit, whose name in the Hebrew tongue is Abaddon, but in the Greek tongue hath his name Apollyon. One woe is past; and, behold, there come two woes more hereafter" (Revelation 9:11,12).

These are not lawless *woes,* and their authors are not disorderly and reckless mobs. They are organized. The strictest obedience to the devil prevails. They are "principalities and powers" of the first order of creation and of great personal power and dignity. They are ordered and sub-ordered, coordinated and subordinated.

They have the most perfect government, military in its discipline, absolute and orderly in its arrangement. They are under one supreme, dictatorial, powerful head, complete with rank and file and officers. "For we wrestle not against flesh and blood, but against principalities, against powers, against the rulers of the darkness of this world, against spiritual wickedness in high places" (Ephesians 6:12).

These high and wicked spirits are everywhere. They fill the air and are intent on evil. They follow the direction of their leader, carrying out his plans with ready obedience and implicit confidence. How loathsome is their nature! How marvelous and miracle-working is their power! How high and kingly is their influence! How military are their purposes!

All this is vividly and strongly set forth in the sixteenth chapter of Revelation: "And I saw three unclean spirits like frogs come out of the mouth of the dragon, and out of the mouth of the beast, and out of the mouth of the false prophet. For they are the spirits of devils, working miracles, which go forth unto the kings of the earth and of the whole world, to gather them to the battle of that great day of God Almighty" (Revelation 16:13,14).

The power of Satan finds its great increase and expression in the efforts and operations of the unregenerate. They are under his power, subjects of his kingdom of darkness. More than that, they are intimate in their connection with Satan, so close in unity, purpose, and relationship that they belong to his family. His paternity gives birth and character to them; his fatherhood binds them in a strong embrace.

## Satan And The Apostles

The power of the devil—it is so defiant, bold, sacreligious, and presumptuous! He came so near the sacred person of Christ! He invaded the sacred circle of His chosen apostles. Judas falls from his high position—tempted, possessed by Satan, and filled with remorse. He commits suicide and hell is his forever.

Peter acts as the spokesman for the devil, becomes the advocate of a non-cross-bearing, non-self-denying, worldly religion. He is so affected by the devil's power that he curses, swears, and lies. Peter finds himself stained and defiled. He is saved only by the prayers of Christ.

John and James fell prey to the devil as they wanted fire to come down from heaven and burn up the Samaritans. Christ sharply shows that they did not have His Spirit, but the other spirit—the spirit of the destroyer.

Paul had his apostolic plans interfered with and hindered by the devil. To the Thessalonians, he writes: "Wherefore we would have come unto you, even I Paul, once and again; but Satan hindered us" (1 Thessalonians 2:18). And he bore to his grave the marks on his body of the power of this ancient foe of apostolic fidelity.

The power of Satan is not supreme. It is limited. This was true in Job's case. Satan could go only so far to afflict him. Since the Son of God came into the world, the devil's power has been curtailed. The cross gave a shock to Satan and his power. His realm of death has been abolished, and "life and immortality (brought) to light through the gospel" (2 Timothy 1:10). His kingdom received its death stroke on Calvary. The almighty forces of the gospel are laying hold of the mighty forces of Satan.

Chapter Eleven

# THE DEVIL'S BATTLEGROUND

*"Now the serpent was more subtle than any beast of the field which the Lord God had made. And he said unto the woman, Yea, hath God said, Ye shall not eat of every tree of the garden? And the woman said unto the serpent, We may eat of the fruit of the trees of the garden: but of the fruit of the tree which is in the midst of the garden, God hath said, Ye shall not eat of it, neither shall ye touch it, lest ye die. And the serpent said unto the woman, Ye shall not surely die: For God doth know that in the day ye eat thereof, then your eyes shall be opened, and ye shall be as gods, knowing good and evil. And when the woman saw that the tree was good for food, and that it was pleasant to the eyes, and a tree to be desired to make one wise, she took of the fruit thereof, and did eat, and gave also unto her husband with her; and he did eat"*—Genesis 3:1-6.

Both in the New Testament and in the Old, the devil is represented as being persistent and tireless in his activities and efforts. In Job, in answer to God's inquiry, "Whence comest thou?" he replies, "From going to and fro in the earth, and from walking up and down in it" (Job 1:7). This statement reveals his rapid and extensive goings and his repeated and careful observations. He is said to be walking about "as a roaring lion" (1 Peter 5:8). Activity, scrutiny, power, and purpose are in his methods.

Thomas a Kempis says: "Know that the ancient enemy doth strive by all means to hinder thy desire to be good and to keep thee clear of all religious exercises. Many evil thoughts does he suggest to thee, that so he may cause a weariness and horror in thee, and to call thee back from prayer and holy reading."

The careless and half-hearted Christian knows nothing about the devil or his devices. But those who serve God are the ones who demand Satan's attention, provoke his anger, and call forth his strategies.

Pastor Blumhart, a marvelous man of faith and power, says: "He who is ignorant of the wiles and artifices of the enemy, only beats the air, and the devil is not afraid of him." Blumhart himself is an illustration. "By concerning myself with a person who was possessed," he says, "I became involved in such a fearful conflict with the powers of darkness that it is not possible for me to describe."

Christians may live and die completely unaware of the devil's existence and hatred. At the same time, Satan is indifferent to their religion because they are not threatening to his kingdom. But a person like Blumhart causes a big commotion and fear in Satan's realm.

## Deceptive Disguises

Satan works by imitation. It is his policy to make something as close to the original as possible and, thereby, break the force and value of the genuine. This is one of his favorite methods. As Jannes and Jambres withstood Moses by their false tricks, so Satan carries on his work by lying wonders. As his apostles are transformed into angels of light, so his wonders are looked on as first class miracles.

What about the revelations of his person? God and Christ have been revealed in bodily shape, by figure, and by representation. Majestic, visible manifestations have been seen by holy men of God. Does the devil have the power to clothe himself in visible form to the human eye? Can he incarnate himself?

Satan seems to have clothed himself in some visible shape at the temptation of Christ. But the form he used is not recorded. Perhaps he appeared in the form of a man, doubtless a pious man. Or maybe he came as a religious hermit from the seclusion of the desert.

In the days of Christ, Satan revealed himself by taking absolute possession of a person and manifested his being and power through other personalities. His manifestations are insidious and deceptive disguises. He sometimes appears as "an angel of light," with the bloom, beauty, and spices of paradise on him. His appearance seems unearthly in splendor, his voice gentle, musical, persuasive, with no traces of the fall.

## Physical Attacks

The devil affects the body and, through the body, affects our loyalty to Christ. Job was tried by his sickness. So the devil tries us by sickness. In the days of Christ, Satan was very active in affecting the body, not simply by ordinary diseases, but by what is termed "possessed with a devil." In those cases, he worked by breaking down some of the body's chief functions.

His method is to assume any shape which will suit his purposes at the time. Doubtless there was something in the shape or character of the serpent which gave him easier access to Eve. Dressed as an angel of light his appearance commends him to those who are pure and unsuspecting.

As a thorn, Satan desires to give only pain to those who, like Paul, cannot be seduced or swerved from the fixed course of fidelity. He puts the Christians at Smyrna in prison and chains their bodies because he could not shackle their souls. With matchless cunning and unspeakable persistence he applies his methods to seduce and damn.

## The Battleground Of The Mind

He has access to the minds of men from which he should forever be barred. But his tricks are so diabolical that he clothes the most sordid act with the fairest guise, and he conceals a world of iniquity with the beautiful colors of the rainbow. He deceived good David and provoked him to number Israel in opposition to God's will, bringing swift and fearful judgment on the nation.

He readily snatches away from the mind any truth which is superficially received. He also blinds the minds of unbelievers and obstructs the light of saving truth. His process of taking the Word out of the heart to prevent faith by blinding the mind to the light of salvation is a very common one.

He makes people sick for the same reasons he made Job sick. He entices men to do wrong and urges them on to evil. He keeps working at it and eats no idle bread. He takes the Word of God out of the unprepared heart and sows tares among the wheat.

The devil goes out into the wilderness, finds us in a fainting, discouraged condition, with our faith weak, the sky cloudy, and our vision obscured. Then he shows us the world from the loftiest peak of observation, clothed in its most attractive form, and tries to ensnare us with its enchanting wonders. He never gets tired of trying to ruin us until the coffin lid is sealed and our happy spirits are bathing in the land where "the wicked cease from troubling; and the weary be at rest" (Job 3:17).

Satan has the wisdom of an archangel and the experience of half an eternity as the captain of all the hosts of hell. He is an expert in the acts and arts of deception and trickery. He has almost inexhaustible resources at his command to serve his purposes. Other than God Himself, a wiser and more powerful spirit than Satan does not live. A more malicious power than he could not exist. There is no greater worker than he. His endless energy and tireless perseverance are the only things in him worthy of imitation. These are the things that make him so powerful and so dreadful.

In the parable of the sower, we are taught how the devil is able to work on the mind and take away any good impressions that are made. "Those by the wayside are they that hear; then cometh the devil, and taketh away the word out of their hearts lest they should not believe and be saved" (Luke 8:12).

We are also taught how the devil influences the mind to do the most wicked things, as in the case of Judas. He was chosen as an apostle, into high and holy fellowship, a royal vocation, a select company. Satan had much to do in influencing Judas to the great crime that brought him to despair and suicide.

## The Devil's Methods

Satan's thorn in the flesh changed Paul's sorrow into joy, his poverty into wealth, his weakness into strength, his reproaches into sweet, heavenly consolations. God must take measures to make Satan's evil deeds work together for good to those who love Him.

As an old saint says, "The devil is but a whetstone to sharpen the faith and patience of the saints." Satan may keep God busy polishing the stones which he makes rough, but the devil's dirt makes their luster brighter, and they become genuine diamonds of the highest quality.

His methods are as varied as the people with whom he deals. The devil knows each person's weaknesses and tendency to sin.

To Eve he came in the disguise of a well-wisher, subtle, serpentine, and deadly. He incites her to disobedience by pointing her to greater heights of godlikeness, along paths of sensual enjoyment. A false and selfish accusation is lodged in her mind against God. No danger is apparent, and he uses no distressing tactics. Instead, he allures, deceives, and ensnares.

The method Satan uses with Job is much different. He was a man of outstanding character, of whom the Lord said, "There is none like him in the earth, a perfect and an upright man, one that feareth God and escheweth evil" (Job 1:8). What methods can Satan devise for this the saintliest of the saints?

Satan goes to God and accuses Job of being selfish in his motives, reducing his piety to the worldly and sinister. No alluring paths, no divergent flowery ways are pointed out to Job, not a word is said to him. Without a note of warning, tragedy and disaster come as an awful surprise and shock. With one desolating blow, his family of ten children are dead, his princely fortune gone, and one dark hour has robbed him of family and possessions. Stripped naked by the fearful rapidity and depth of his losses, he becomes homeless, childless, and friendless. His grief is inconsolable and the darkness impenetrable.

The integrity of Job is like a marble column blackened by the smoke. He is unshaken by the fiery ordeal but still pursued by the devil. Still Satan insinuates and maligns the genuineness of Job's piety.

He does not recognize Job's noble fidelty or lofty loyalty. Satan continues to attribute low motives as the reason for Job's integrity. With heartless cruelty and malicious lies, he pursues his death-dealing work.

Out of his arsenal of hellish weapons, he comes with a loathsome disease. He concentrates on this one saint, affliction on affliction, until his wife is alienated, his friends estranged, his enemies triumphant. There is no relief for his hopeless, bitter grief. His pious reputation has been blackened, his body tortured, his mind put in agony. This is another of Satan's methods: to distress and defame those whom he cannot deceive.

## The Deadliest Disguise

To the Son of God in the wilderness, Satan did not come as he came to Job in frustrating storms of distress, but in the form of apparent sympathy and friendliness. It may have been in the disguise of a saintly hermit in the wilderness. "If Thou be the Son of God"—You want this matter of Your Sonship to God settled, and so do I. You are very hungry and faint—"Command that these stones be made bread" (Matthew 4:3). This appears to be an innocent and proper way to quickly settle a great question and appease great hunger.

Then Satan comes to Christ and tempts Him with the sanctity of the temple. He gives Him an opportunity to attest His Messiahship before the wondering and awe-struck worshippers assembled there. This seems to be a shorter and better way to give credence to His mission than the slow and thankless process of daily teaching and ministering. It would appear to be easier than marching to the cross with the dark shadows of its shame and heaviness darkening His way.

Satan's desperate venture was to seduce Christ by the world's array of grandeur, power, and glory. Satan plunged Job from a serene, cloudless, heavenly height down to a starless and stormy midnight. To the Son of God, Satan would be an available friend to save Him from pain, poverty, hunger, shame, toil, and death.

Chapter Twelve

# SATAN'S CLEVER STRATEGIES

*"But if our gospel be hid, it is hid to them that are lost: in whom the god of this world hath blinded the minds of them which believe not, lest the light of the glorious gospel of Christ, who is the image of God, should shine unto them. . .For God, who commanded the light to shine out of darkness, hath shined in our hearts, to give the light of the knowledge of the glory of God in the face of Jesus Christ. . .We are troubled on every side, yet not distressed; we are perplexed, but not in despair; persecuted, but not forsaken; cast down, but not destroyed"*—2 Corinthians 4:3,4,6-9.

The devil is rarely seen in his movements and methods. He has the rare ability to get others to do his work and execute his plans.

His methods are to blind, to put a veil on the evil results and all the sad consequences of sin. He blinds people so that the evil cannot be seen. Even David, who loved God, was blinded by Satan to the treachery, infamy, and murder in Uriah's case.

This is how sinners are held in unbelief by Satan. He closes their eyes to all the light and glory of the shining Son of Righteousness. "In whom the god of this world hath blinded the minds of them which believe not, lest the light of the glorious gospel of Christ, who is the image of God, should shine unto them" (2 Corinthians 4:4).

## Blinded Minds

The power of the devil extends to the mind. He can influence the mind, insinuate thoughts, suggest purposes, and excite the imagination. Satan can inflame the passions, stir the appetites, awaken old habits, and fan dead flames or light new ones. He deceived the natural innocence of Eve. He entered into Judas, possessed him fully, and made his half-formed treason complete.

Satan was involved in the private council of Ananias and Sapphira, a party to their fraud. He suggested their lying plan to deceive the apostles. His access to the mind is evident in that he snatches away the divine seed implanted in the soil of the heart as taught in the parable of the sower.

In Corinthians, the devil is called *the god of this world*. "The god of this world hath blinded the minds of them which believe not, lest the light of the glorious gospel of Christ, who is the image of God, should shine unto them."

The devil uses this world as a veil to shut out the truth of God and the light of His glorious gospel. He closes the eyes of faith to all the discoveries in the unseen and eternal.

The antagonism between the children of the world who are possessed by Satan and the children of God who are possessed by God is set forth by John. "Ye are of God, little children, and have overcome them: because greater is He that is in you, than he that is in the world. They are of the world: therefore speak they of the world, and the world heareth them. We are of God: he that knoweth God heareth us; he that is not of God heareth not us. Hereby know we the spirit of truth, and the spirit of error" (1 John 4:4-6).

Who is in us? God. Who is in the children of the world? The devil. Our faith, our hope, and our final triumph are in the truth of the Word of God. "Greater is He that is in us than he that is in the world."

Satan perverts the things which are truly works of God and misemploys miracles to obscure God's glory.

## Fear And Discouragement

The devil often tries to break the soul down and reduce it to despair. In order to discourage us, he tells us that we will never succeed. The way is too hard and the burden too heavy.

He takes advantage of weak, distracted nerves and suggests fears. Grace is hidden from sight, shortcomings are magnified, and weaknesses are classed as gross sins. Sometimes the fear of death is used by Satan to quench the fire of faith, and the grave becomes something awful.

He darkens the future. Heaven and God are hidden by a thick veil of tomorrow's cares, trials, and needs. The imaginary disasters, failures, and evils of the future are powerful weapons in Satan's hand. He suggests that the Lord is a hard master and that His promises will fail. He works on the remaining corruption in the heart and raises a great storm in the soul.

Samuel Rutherford says: "Oh, if our faith could ride out against the high and proud waves and winds when our sea seemeth all on fire! Oh, how oft do I let my grips go. I am put to swimming and half sinking. I find the devil has the advantage in this battle, for he fighteth in known ground for our corruption. However matters go, it is our happiness to win new grounds daily in Christ's love and to add conquest to conquest until our Lord Jesus and we are so near each other that Satan cannot draw a straw or a thread between us."

## Temptations And Feelings

He tempts us to lash out with evil tempers, to speak hasty words, and to be impatient. He tempts us to use carnal reasoning which is his powerful ally in our minds. We must turn back to Christ. We need more of His Spirit-renewed commitment and thorough self-dedication. By sending prayers upward with an uplifted eye and heart, we will be able to resist and conquer the great adversary of our souls.

One of the most intelligent and God-honored among the saints wrote: "I have keen inward sufferings, what are termed the buffetings of Satan.

Horror at times has taken hold of me. I felt much, but feared more.''

The devil may tempt us to think too little of ourselves as Moses did and too highly of ourselves as Peter did. In one sense, we cannot think too little of ourselves, but in another way we can. Satan persuades us that we are so poor and weak we can do nothing. And so we are weakened in faith and broken in effort. But his master method is to fill us with self-importance and self-confidence. And then not only is faith weakened but destroyed. Our efforts and activities may increase in number and vain exhibition, but the seal of self and Satan are on them all.

John Wesley notes: ''I preached on that delicate device of Satan to destroy the whole religion of the heart. Telling Christians not to regard feelings, but to live by naked faith, is in plain terms, not to regard either love, joy, peace, or any other fruit of the Spirit; not to regard whether they feel them or the reverse; whether their souls be in a heavenly or hellish frame of mind. Satan's method with some is to make them rely too much on feelings. With others he deals the reverse and urges them to discard all feelings.''

Naked faith is often nothing but fruitless, unconscious acceptance that brings fruitless, unconscious salvation with it, if it brings salvation at all.

## All Power

Whatever Satan's methods or clever devices, the

words of Jesus, his conqueror, to us are these: "Behold, I give unto you power to tread on serpents and scorpions, and over all the power of the enemy: and nothing shall by any means hurt you" (Luke 10:19).

Miss Havergal writes concerning these verses: "Why, this is grand—*power over all the power* of the enemy. Just where he is strongest there they shall prevail. Not over the very center of his power, not over his power here and there, nor now and then, but over *all* his power. And Jesus said, 'Is not that enough to go into battle with?' "

The devil's brain is prolific with plans. He has many ways of doing many things. Perhaps he has many ways of doing each thing. With him nothing is stereotyped. He never runs in ruts. Fruitful, diverse, and ever-fresh is his way of doing things. Indirect, cunning, and graceful are his plans. He acts by trickery and always by guile.

According to the Bible, his plans are "wiles." The original word means to follow up or investigate by method and settled plan. It is not a bad word but one of order, arrangement, and methods which are conceived and executed. But when the word gets into the devil's hand, it is defined by his dictionary. It receives a strong stain, a deep coloring of cunning and trickery.

Sometimes Satan comes to us disrobed of his heavenly garments. He comes as a sharp, pointed, painful, poisoned thorn—a thorn that cannot be extracted by prayer. The saints who have seen most of heaven are often summoned to see most of hell. Saints who have the fullest and most transporting revelation of God often have the saddest experience with Satan.

Paul's thorn meant as much to Paul as his abundance of revelations. His thorn made him more a saint than his vision of the third heavens. Satan only lifted him higher by keeping him lower.

Satan may come to us in his own native character, the thorn breeder and piercer. He may put thorns in us which no prayer power can extract—thorns which will poison and pain. But the thorn will enrich grace, increase humility, and make weakness strong and glorious. Satan's thorns will clothe necessities with richest attire; change distresses and persecutions into the most divine pleasures.

Satan's thorns will make room for God's greatest power in us and on us. The enemy's thorns will make the lowest point of a spiritual depression the highest point of vision. And his thorns will make strength out of weakness and wealth out of poverty.

# Chapter Thirteen

# OUR MOST VULNERABLE AREAS

*"To whom ye forgive any thing, I forgive also: for if I forgave any thing, to whom I forgave it, for your sakes forgave I it in the person of Christ: lest Satan should get an advantage of us: for we are not ignorant of his devices"*—2 Corinthians 2:10,11.

There are positions and conditions which lie open to the attacks of Satan. These points must be guarded by sleepless vigilance. The devil is a cruel and mighty foe. To watch him with unsleeping eye is not only a duty, but essential to life. Deliverance from hell and the certainty of heaven are involved in overcoming the devil. Stupidity, neglect, and being off guard in the conflict with Satan are much more than mistakes or indiscretions. They are fatal defeats—eternal and irreparable losses.

The apostle places his Corinthian brethren on the winning side in the war with the devil by declaring, "We are not ignorant of Satan's devices." *Ignorance is always an exposed condition.* Ignorance is open to attack and surprise by day and by night. To be ignorant of the existence, character, and ways of the devil is the prelude to fatal results in the fight for heaven. If this is true, how hopeless is the case of one who is not only ignorant of the temptations, but denies or ignores the existence of the tempter.

The devil's great device, his masterpiece of temptation, is to destroy faith in his own existence. God's struggle is to establish faith in His own existence. The devil's great work is to eradicate all spiritual facts, principles, and persons—good or evil, God and the devil. He who denies or ignores the existence of the devil puts up a fatal barrier to ultimate salvation and paralyzes all efforts in that direction. This ignorance gives one over, chained hand and foot, to the merciless foe whose existence has been denied and derided.

Nothing advances Satan's work with more skillful hands than to be ignorant of Satan and his ways. To escape his snare, we must have a strong faith in the fact that Satan exists. We must also have an intimate knowledge of him and his plans.

## Taking The Devil Lightly

Related to the foregoing vulnerable position is the one which makes light of Satan—frivolous views of him, his works, or his character. Light talk or jokes that dishonor him are detrimental to any serious views of life's great work and its serious conflicts. Presumption, self-will, and foolishness are the characteristics of those who deal frivolously with these important concerns.

The existence and work of the devil is a serious matter. It is to be considered and dealt with from the most serious standpoint, and only serious people can deal with it. For this reason, the New Testament gives the repeated note of warning, "be sober." The point is emphatically made in the statement, "Be sober. . .because your adversary the devil. . ." (1 Peter 1:8).

Related to this attitude is Jude's incisive and almost rough handling of those who make light of sacred things and sacred persons: "Likewise also these filthy dreamers defile the flesh, despise dominion, and speak evil of dignities. Yet Michael the archangel, when contending with the devil he disputed about the body of Moses, durst not bring against him a railing accusation, but said, The Lord rebuke thee. But these speak evil of those things which they know not; but what they know naturally, as brute beasts, in those things they corrupt themselves" (Jude 10).

Peter also has something to say about this same class of flippant, irreverent talkers: "Presumptuous are they, self-willed, they are not afraid to speak evil of dignities. Whereas angels, which are greater in power and might, bring not railing accusation against them before the Lord. But these, as natural brute beasts, made to be taken and destroyed, speak evil of the things that they understand not; and shall utterly perish in their own corruption; and shall receive the reward of unrighteousness, as they that count it pleasure to riot in the day time. Spots they are and blemishes, sporting themselves with their own deceivings while they feast with you" (2 Peter 2:10-13).

A paralyzing attitude in which we remain to listen to Satan's insinuations is fatal. This was Eve's mistake. His tongue is smooth as oil, his words circulate and inflame like poison. For this reason, our position must be one of bristling opposition, fortified for war, with no barriers down, no open gates, no low places. Fenced in and barricaded against the devil is the only safe place.

## An Unforgiving Spirit

An unforgiving spirit invites Satanic possession. His favorite realm is the spirit. To corrupt our spirit, to provoke us to retaliation, revenge, or unmercifulness—that is his chosen work and his most common and successful device. Paul brings this device out into the open so we can thwart Satan's plans. "To whom ye forgive any thing, I forgive also: for if I forgave any thing, to whom I forgave it, for your sakes forgave I it in the person of Christ; lest Satan should get an advantage of us: for we are not ignorant of his devices" (2 Corinthians 2:10,11).

When Satan generates an unforgiving spirit in us, then he has us, and we are on his ground. Then wicked men and good men, all kinds of people, are likely to do us harm, sometimes at vital and very sensitive points. Sometimes they unconsciously wrong us and sometimes they do it knowingly and willfully. As soon as a spirit of unkindness possesses us for the wrong done to us, Satan has the upper hand.

## Oaths And Swearing

We quote the warning words of our Savior: "Again, ye have heard that it hath been said by them of old time, Thou shalt not forswear thyself, but shalt perform unto the Lord thine oaths: But I say unto you, Swear not at all; neither by heaven; for it is God's throne: Nor by the earth; for it is His footstool: neither by Jerusalem; for it is the city of the great King. Neither shalt thou swear by thy head, because thou canst not make one hair white or black. But let your communication be, Yea, yea; Nay, nay: for whatsoever is more than these cometh of evil (or the evil one)" (Matthew 5:33-37).

The injunction is against using strong oaths in language. Expletives and appeals added to our words are wrong and expose us to the snare of Satan. "In the multitude of words," says Proverbs, "there wanteth not sin" (Proverbs 10:19).

Satan tempts us to use assertions and declarations to confirm the truth of what we are saying. When we use additional words as a way of substantiating the truth of those already spoken, they expose us to Satan's power. "But above all things, my brethren, swear not, neither by heaven, neither by the earth, neither by any other oath: but let your yea be yea; and your nay, nay; lest ye fall into condemnation" (James 5:12). James seals the words of Christ. The devil lies concealed in many words. Simplicity, brevity, and seriousness of words will mightily hinder and thwart his ensnaring plans.

It is so easy for the devil to stop us just short of a faith that will save. There are many speeches, prefaces, and introductions which are sometimes quite monotonous. They are often headed in the right direction, but they do not bring us to the heart of the matter. Like Sarah, they start with full intent to go to Canaan, but stop at Haran and dwell there. Like Jacob, Schechem slows their steps and holds them instead of Bethel.

## Religious Fanaticism

On the other hand, there are those who are earnestly striving after that "holiness without which no man shall see the Lord." Satan tempts them to go a little too far and their zeal degenerates into ungodly fervor that causes division in the Church.

Strict earnestness degenerates into severity and gentleness into weakness. Energetic activity turns into imprudent meddling and narrowness. Calm moderation soon becomes careless acquiesence. Bold convictions become intolerant, opinionated, and bigoted. Respect for the convictions of others degenerates into paralyzing indifference and skeptical laziness. Eager trust lapses into presumption and haughtiness. Cautious wisdom soon becomes cowardice and hesitating anxiety. Confession and profession evaporate into dry religious duty.

Satan watches and is always alert to try to hold us back from the final goal. Or he works in the opposite way to drive us on with an impetuous and obsessed spirit to go beyond the goal. It is Satan's purpose to uncover our strongest positions and turn them into vulnerable areas.

## Being Unequally Yoked

Becoming unequally yoked with unbelievers in intimate and confiding friendships creates exposed positions of which the devil takes great advantage. Partnership in business or the more sacred union of marriage with unbelievers is perilous to the believer in Jesus Christ.

"Be ye not unequally yoked together with unbelievers: for what fellowship hath righteousness with unrighteousness? and what communion hath light with darkness? And what concord hath Christ with Belial?" (2 Corinthians 6:14,15).

Satan is called Belial which means someone who is worthless, contemptible, and wicked. He and Christ cannot be joined in agreement. No unequal yoking, no fellowship, no communion, no agreement can exist. The result is contamination and impurity. The fruit of these voluntary close yokings is a weakened spiritual condition. Under the law, an ox and an ass could not be yoked together. Under the Spirit, Christ and Satan can have no agreements.

Separation, cleansing, and perfected holiness are necessary to secure the vantage ground against Satan. The Bible gives strong, explicit, and comprehensive commands against union, communion, or intimate association with unbelievers. For those unequally yoked there can be no pulling together, no fellowship, no sharing, no communion, no intimacy, no agreement, no voting together.

Commentators have found in these verses from 2 Corinthians, Paul's fine command of the Greek language. We find in them the fire of fervent and profound convictions. They demand self-denying abstinence from forming intimate and voluntary associations with the unbelieving world in business, pleasure, or social pursuits.

Paul laid down this rule in his first epistle to the Corinthians: "I wrote unto you in an epistle not to company with fornicators: Yet not altogether with the fornicators of this world, or with the covetous, or extortioners, or with idolaters; for then must ye needs go out of the world. But now I have written unto you not to keep company, if any man that is called a brother be a fornicator, or covetous, or an idolator, or a railer, or a drunkard, or an extortioner; with such a one no not to eat" (1 Corinthians 5:11). Paul is not objecting to casual, courteous Christian conversation but to more intimate and lasting relationships.

## Worldly Friendships

James defines and opposes these worldly relationships and attachments as vulnerable positions which result in the most criminal violation of the holiest relationship. "Ye adulterers and adulteresses, know ye not that the friendship of the world is enmity with God? whosoever therefore will be a friend of the world is the enemy of God" (James 4:4). By such associations, the marriage vow of

God is broken.

Dean Alford, commenting on this passage, says: "Of the world, it means men and men's interest, ambitions and employments, in so far as they are without God. The man who is taken out of the world by Christ cannot again become the friend and companion of worldly men and their schemes, without passing into enmity with God. God and the world stand opposed to one another, so that a man cannot join the one without deserting the other. He, therefore, who desires to be the friend of the world, and sets his mind and thought and wish that way, must make up his mind to be God's enemy."

We may ask, "But shouldn't I be friendly with my relatives whether they fear God or not?" There is nothing we can do to change our family relationships, but there are some which are nearer to us than others. The nearest relatives are husbands and wives. They have taken each other for better or worse, and they must make the best of each other. God has joined them together, and no one can put them asunder.

Parents are also very closely connected with their children. You cannot part with them while they are young, because it is your duty to "train them up in the way wherein they should go." Once they are grown your relationship with them changes, and you must use your own discretion to determine how close you will be to them.

Children must also determine how long it is expedient for them to remain with their parents.

In general, if they do not fear God, you should leave them as soon as is convenient.

As for all other relatives, even brothers or sisters, if they are of the world, you are under no obligation to be closely associated with them. You may be courteous and friendly, but at a distance.

## The Only Escape

Since "friendship of the world is enmity against God," the only way to heaven is to avoid all intimacy with worldly people. Whatever the cost, flee spiritual adultery! Have no friendship with the world. No matter how tempted you are by profit or pleasure, do not become intimate with worldly-minded people. And if you are already involved with anyone who is of the world, break it off without delay.

Your life is at stake—eternal life or eternal death. Is it not better to go into life having one eye or one hand, than having both, to be cast into hell-fire? No matter how tempted you are to continue, have no friendship with the world. Look around and see the dreadful effects it has produced among your brethren! How many of the mighty have fallen because of this very thing! They would heed no warning. They conversed intimately with worldly-minded people until they themselves were back in the world again.

Oh, "come out from among them!" (2 Corinthians 6:17). Come out from all unholy men, however harmless they may appear, "and be ye separate"—at least have no intimacy with them. Your "fellowship is with the Father, and with His Son Jesus Christ" (1 John 1:3). So let your fellowship be with those, and those only, who at least seek the Lord Jesus Christ in sincerity. So "shall ye be," in a peculiar sense, "My sons and My daughters, saith the Lord Almighty" (2 Corinthians 6:18).

How Satan surrounds us! How strongly he holds us! How he entangles, chains, and binds us with worldly associations! We lie in the sweet friendship, the embraces, and counsel of these worldly ones, while they lie in the arms of the wicked one.

## A Simple Answer

If *simplicity* is removed from our faith, our defenses against Satan are weakened. "I am jealous over you with godly jealousy: for I have espoused you to one husband, that I may present you as a chaste virgin to Christ. But I fear, lest by any means as the serpent beguiled Eve through his subtility, so your minds should be corrupted from the simplicity that is in Christ" (2 Corinthians 11:2,3).

Satan is recognized as the serpent who is still busy at his old tricky trade. Satan has such a dexterous and successful hand at deception that Paul was uneasy. Lack of simplicity could be fatal to the purity and faith of the Corinthians, just as the taste of the forbidden fruit was fatal to Eve. It was the loss of a little thing, but, with it, all was lost.

## The Importance Of Discipline

An *undisciplined body* readily exposes us to

Satan's assaults. Even natural, innocent appetites and passions have to be held in with bit and bridle. Paul was aware of this: "But I keep under my body, and bring it into subjection: lest that by any means, when I have preached to others, I myself should be a castaway" (1 Corinthians 9:27). An undisciplined body could hurl Paul from the office of an apostle down to the fearful abyss of apostasy.

Two statements are made in reference to his body: "keep under" and "bring it into subjection." The first means a blow to that part of the face under the eyes. If something is restrained and suppressed by heavy blows its power is broken.

The second statement, "bring it into subjection," means to make a slave of, to treat with severity, to subject to stern and rigid discipline. The apostle sees the body as an important factor in the contest for heaven. He teaches us that if it is untrained, without the strong repressing hand of discipline, it becomes an easy prey to the assaults of Satan.

Peter gives the same directions: "Be sober, be vigilant; because your adversary the devil, as a roaring lion, walketh about, seeking whom he may devour: Whom resist steadfast in the faith, knowing that the same afflictions are accomplished in your brethren that are in the world" (1 Peter 5:8,9). A listless, drowsy, sleepy, stupid state can put us under Satan's power without a struggle or even the decency of a surrender.

Remember the strong injuction of Christ to the drowsy and fainting disciples: "Watch and pray, that ye enter not into temptation: the spirit indeed is willing, but the flesh is weak'' (Matthew 26:41).

Chapter Fourteen

# WHERE DOES SATAN ATTACK?

*"This is a true saying, If a man desire the office of a bishop, he desireth a good work. A bishop then must be blameless, the husband of one wife, vigilant, sober, of good behaviour, given to hospitality, apt to teach; not given to wine, no striker, not greedy of filthy lucre; but patient, not a brawler, not covetous; one that ruleth well. . .not a novice, lest being lifted up with pride he fall into the condemnation of the devil. Moreover he must have a good report of them which are without; lest he fall into reproach and the snare of the devil"*—1 Timothy 3:1-4,6-7.

We have two statements in first Timothy regarding the appointing of men to active and official leadership in the Church. The first statement is against appointing novices to such leadership. "Not a novice, lest being lifted up with pride he fall into the condemnation of the devil" (1 Timothy 3:6).

To put immature believers in places of spiritual leadership causes them to become filled with pride. If the young convert is put into a highly visible position, he readily falls into the same condemnation into which the devil fell because of pride. This text from 1 Timothy gives credence to the Church's almost universally accepted opinion: that the devil fell through pride.

New converts must be matured by discipline before they are put to the front. Staying behind is often a greater cross, as well as a greater virtue, than pushing or being pushed to the front. The forefront is always an unsafe place for faith until faith has grown and matured.

Men of questionable reputation who are placed in church leadership or official positions bring reproach and help the devil in his disgraceful business. "Moreover he must have a good report of them which are without; lest he fall into reproach and the snare of the devil" (1 Timothy 3:7). Having men of good character and spotless reputation in the leadership of church affairs closes Satan's mouth, cuts off his revenue, and slows down his business.

We must not violate these two rules of church government by putting novices and men whose reputation is not spotless in positions of leadership. It puts the novices in an uncomfortable position, and it increases the dangerous influence of leaders who have questionable reputations. The entire Church is also put in an exposed condition, endangering the whole army.

Leaders are standard bearers whose lives are clearly visible to everyone in the Church. For this reason they should be conspicuous in spotless piety. They should be mature in age, sound and advanced in faith, love, and sobriety. Gifted, wise, serious, and blameless leaders will make the Church strong and victorious in the day of battle.

Novices in the position of church leadership create conditions exposed to Satan's attacks. New converts should be sheltered and trained before they are given any responsibility in the local church.

## The Devil's Workshop

Young widowhood can also be a vulnerable condition in the Church. Satan is always watching for any opportunity to invade the vulnerable position of the grieving widow. Paul knew the hidden traps that Satan often uses.

Paul writes tenderly, honestly, and with discrimination: "Honour widows that are widows indeed. But if any widow have children or nephews, let them learn first to shew piety at home, and to requite their parents: for that is good and acceptable before God. Now she that is a widow indeed, and desolate, trusteth in God, and continueth in supplications and prayers night and day. But she that liveth in pleasure is dead while she liveth. . . .But the younger widows refuse: for when they have begun to wax wanton against Christ, they will marry, having damnation, because they have cast off their first faith. And withal they learn to be idle, wandering about from house to house; and not only idle, but tattlers also and busybodies, speaking things which they ought not. I will therefore that the younger women marry, bear children, guide the house, give none occasion to the adversary to speak reproachfully. For some are already turned aside after Satan" (1 Timothy 5:3-6,11-15).

This advice helps relieve the sorrow of the young woman and puts her where her heart and hands are full of sweet and sacred responsibilities. Her time and heart are full of profitable activity. Satan has a hard job working on a person who is filled in heart and hands with the holy tasks of raising the home, state, and Church of the future.

### The Problem Of Lust

There are strong natural desires in man which the Scriptures term *lust*. They are called "lusts of the flesh," "lusts of the eye," "worldly lusts," and the "lusts of men." These are the cravings of the senses for which the heart naturally clamors.

These lusts form the basis of inner temptation. A cunning and powerful seducer may tempt and lead an innocent person astray when there is no inward response to his allurements. But these inner lusts and desires form the basis and provide the ground-work for Satan's insidious temptations.

James describes the whole process: "Let no man say when he is tempted, I am tempted of God for God cannot be tempted with evil, neither tempteth He any man: But every man is tempted, when he is drawn away of his own lust, and enticed. Then when lust hath conceived, it bringeth forth sin: and sin, when it is finished, bringeth forth death" (James 1:13-15).

The term "drawn away" means to "lure forth." The metaphor is from hunting or fishing. As game is lured from the forests, so man by lust is allured from the safety of self-restraint to sin. The word "enticed" means to catch with bait.

The Scriptures demand that these lusts or desires be banned and denounced. We can see how Satan and the world are behind these lusts. The gospel is a training school in which these lusts are to be denied. "For the grace of God that bringeth salvation hath appeared to all men, teaching us that, denying ungodliness and worldy lusts, we should live soberly, righteously, and godly in this present world" (Titus 2:11,12).

This solemn declaration from Titus is made without qualification or deception. It is a declarative statement carrying the force of an imperative demand and also that of a condition: "And they that are Christ's have crucified the flesh with the affections and lusts" (Galatians 5:24).

The work of Christ is presented as a pattern for us to copy in destroying these lusts: "Forasmuch then as Christ hath suffered for us in the flesh, arm yourselves likewise with the same mind: for he that hath suffered in the flesh hath ceased from sin; that he no longer should live the rest of his time in the flesh to the lusts of men, but to the will of God" (1 Peter 4:1,2).

We are taught that these lusts are put in opposition to the will of God. They cannot be yielded to and remain in obedience to God. No man can serve these two masters. These lusts are the basis and sources of corruption. They war against the soul. We are to "put off concerning the former conversation the old man, which is corrupt according to the deceitful lusts; and be renewed in the spirit of your mind; and that ye put on the new man, which after God is created in righteousness and true holiness" (Ephesians 4:22-24).

## A Weakened Position

The war with Satan is concerned about these lusts. This lusting after the pleasures of the senses is not completely destroyed when we are converted to Christ. It is broken in power and weakened, but the remains, the roots, are still there. Like a tree in life, cut down at its stump, they send up many shoots. If we allow these shoots to remain, they will help Satan in his work.

Those who are content to leave the remains of these lusts inside them will be hampered by an internal struggle. To allow sin or the tendency to sin to remain in us is fatal. It is as fatal as leaving the original natives in the land of Canaan was to the piety, peace, and prosperity of Israel. God's command to Israel was that those nations were to be destroyed completely so as to leave neither root nor branch. Israel's failure to do this was the source of untold evil for them.

Any remaining lusts are exposed conditions just as the remains of a decayed tooth are the exposed conditions of a toothache. So we are challenged,

"For if ye live after the flesh, ye shall die: but if ye through the Spirit do mortify the deeds of the body, ye shall live" (Romans 8:13).

In another text, we have these words: "They that are Christ's have crucified the flesh, with its affections and lusts" (Galatians 5:24). "Lust" is the larger word in Scripture, including the whole world of active lusts and desires. The "affections" are not so much the soul's disease in its more active operations, but the diseased conditions out of which these spring.

The lusts spring from the passions and are nourished by them. They deserve the same punishment as the flesh. All of these—the flesh, the lusts, and affections—are crucified. This puts the Christian in the best fortified condition to resist the attacks of the devil. If these lusts remain, he is only half armed and wholly exposed.

## Lack Of Spiritual Growth

Low aims in the spiritual life and satisfaction with present circumstances create an exposed condition. The devil may *visit* the highlands and mountain ranges of spiritual elevation, but he makes his *home* in the lowlands. He will attack the strongest, most mature giant of piety. But he works his havoc and gains his spoils where the Christian slumbers in the cradle of spiritual babyhood. There is only safety in high aims, strenuous effort, and constant advance.

It is on the field of low aims and satisfied results that the devil wins his chief victories. Spiritual growth along with constant and sure spiritual development is the surest safeguard against Satan's assaults and surprises. Constant growth keeps our eyes open and our hearts strong. Satan never finds growth asleep, drowsy, or weak. Onward and upward is the great battle cry. Constant advance is the steel armor in the fight with the devil.

Israel lost Canaan by not possessing Canaan. Satan has the vantage ground when we do not maintain an aggressive forward march.

When the Bible sounded the clarion call, "Let us go unto perfection" (Hebrews 6:1), it was seeking to arouse the Church. The believers had lost the vigor and fighting ability of Christian character by feeding on milk and indulging in the lazy luxury of being children. The Scriptures raise a standard and set a goal for them to attain. The goal line is far ahead, but it is a real point, as real as the point at which their steps were delayed. They are called out of the cradle and away from the nursery to the strength, conflict, and perfection of royal maturity.

A great writer said of Wesley that he was "the first of theological statesmen." This is no great compliment. But the spiritual perception of Wesley as a man of open, divine vision is his highest eulogy. This is evidenced by the fact that he reechoed the trumpet call of the Bible and sounded it on every key and in every refrain. He sought to stir the Church into forward movement and quicken its members to seek an advanced position. The yearning for spiritual growth had diminished in their experience and had been left out of their hopes and creeds.

God gives the beginning and these beginnings are glorious. But to be content with the beginnings of faith forfeits its possibilities and leaves us open and naked to Satan. Then we become a prey to his schemes.

Making additions to our spiritual treasury is the essential condition for stability in the Christian life. Retaining and maintaining this stability gives great victory over the devil. To stand still in our faith is to lose it. To set up camp at the place of salvation is to forfeit regenerating grace. To stop at any station of progress is to go backward. The weakness of most people is their lack of determination to stick to their objective. We are willing to pay the personal cost for great temporal success, but the price is often too dear for spiritual success.

## Baby Christians

The tendency in religion is to be satisfied with spiritual birth and then to die in infancy. The teething phase is a perilous time for spiritual babes. The great sin of the Israelites was hugging the shores and not going up to possess the land. The marvelous glory of their entrance into Canaan was diminished by the lethargy and timidity of their advance.

Stopping and standing still in a non-growing, non-fighting condition is a position fully exposed to Satan. Many run well and fight well, but at some point their running and fighting cease. When this happens, spiritual development is arrested, and the devil moves at once to an easy victory.

This spiritual arrest may happen during the initial steps or stages of spiritual life. The excitement and triumphs of the first stages may arrest advance and cause a standstill. This may happen before the cradle is out of sight and while the first steps of the Christian toddler are still unsteady.

It is true that Paul calls the Corinthian saints baby saints. But this was at the point where their saintship turned back to carnality and lost its sanctity and strength. Their great sin and backslidings were found in their babyhood; not that they began as babes, but that they stayed babes. Baby Christianity is the popular Christianity of these days. To begin as babes is expected, but to remain babes for forty years is a fearful deformity.

Spiritual stagnation sometimes happens to those in the high echelons of spiritual prominence. It is true that a few of those who have received a great spiritual baptism after conversion have crystallized around this point of advance. However, a far greater number of people and preachers have crystallized around the initial experience of salvation. There may be some specimens of Christian mummies who approached maturity, but the number who were petrified in the dwarfed and cradled state is countless.

## Spiritual Stagnation

However, spiritual stagnation is not confined to

the initial steps. Its life-blood may chill and its step halt at the point of highest advance. Many Christians are so enthusiastic over some marked advance, or some higher elevation gained, that they become enchanted with the beautiful and lofty regions. They are lulled to sleep and, like Bunyan's Pilgrim, lose their enthusiasm and are unconscious of their loss. Instead of pressing on with tireless steps, they cover the future with their imaginations. Then, while their minds are filled with fantasies of their advanced position, their feet have slipped backward, and they are in the valley again. They are so happy that it is almost impossible to bring them to their senses.

It is difficult to make them understand that there are many weary and toilsome steps between their Red Sea deliverance and the promised land. Even after the desert is crossed, the Jordon divided, and their feet touched the sanctified soil of Canaan, there are many battles to be fought. There are enemies to be destroyed before the good land is all possessed.

It is good to have singing and shouting sanctification. But if it is not joined by marching and fighting faith, it will sing and shout itself as thin as a ghost and as dry as a desert. "Forgetting those things which are behind, and reaching forth unto those things which are before" (Philippians 3:13). This is the divine process by which we hold onto what we have by getting more.

Paul's marvelous career was simple, not complex. He sums it up as fighting, running, watching—the three elements of continuous advance. Many great battles have been lost by the demoralizing effects of the halt caused by a partial victory in the earlier part of the conflict. It is not easy to keep in place and march in rank when the spoils of a half-gained victory cover the ground. There is no position this side of heaven that is free from the dangers of spiritual arrest and secure from the devil's attacks. The conflict and vigilance of advance must mark every step until our feet are within the pearly gates.

Arrested spiritual development in the initial stages, or at the more advanced, is always an exposed position. Spiritual immaturity always leaves us vulnerable to Satan's attacks.

Chapter Fifteen

# USING OUR DEFENSES

*"And unto the angel of the church in Sardis write: These things saith he that hath the seven Spirits of God, and the seven stars; I know thy works, that thou hast a name that thou livest, and art dead. Be watchful, and strengthen the things which remain, that are ready to die: for I have not found thy works perfect before God. Remember therefore how thou hast received and heard, and hold fast, and repent. If therefore thou shalt not watch, I will come on thee as a thief, and thou shalt not know what hour I will come upon thee. Thou hast a few names even in Sardis which have not defiled their garments; and they shall walk with me in white: for they are worthy. He that overcometh, the same shall be clothed in white raiment; and I will not blot out his name out of the book of life, but I will confess his name before my Father, and before his angels"*—Revelation 3:1-5.

Leave no room for the devil. Be too busy for him. Have no time and no place for him. Vacant places invite him. The devil loves a vacuum. A very busy person himself, he does his biggest business with those who have no business.

The apostle, in writing to the Ephesians, gives this direction: "Neither give place to the devil" (4:27). Leave no opening, no space for him. Keep him out by prepossession. Keep him out—nose, head, and all. Give him an inch and he will take a mile.

"Give no place to the devil." The apostle is writing about how anger can cause us to give full scope to the devil. He comes into power and has full sway when we relinquish ourselves to the indulgence and continuance of evil passion. Our evil passions are the regions where Satan finds his favorite field and largest sphere of operation. Suppress evil and every tendency to indignation, bitterness, and wrath. Suppress and purge out every heated impulse, every unholy desire, every feeling that is not of God. The devil's work is futile when gentleness and forgiveness reign in our spirit.

"Resist the devil and he will flee from you" (James 4:7). This is James' curt directory for getting rid of the devil. Resist means to set one's self against, to withstand. Yield nothing to him at any point, but oppose him at every point. Always be against him, belonging to the party of the opposition as far as his plans, suggestions, and ways are concerned.

If we bravely and strongly resist what the devil proposes, the victory is half won. To hesitate is to lose. To talk it over is to yield, to give an inch is to surrender the whole ground. The devil cannot stand firmness, decision, and opposition. He is easily defeated if we are determined and uncompromising. Loyalty to God is ruin to Satan.

## How To Resist The Devil

We are taught this same simple, important lesson in Peter, along with an addition: "Be sober, be vigilant; because your adversary the devil, as a roaring lion, walketh about, seeking whom he may devour: whom resist steadfast in the faith, knowing that the same afflictions are accomplished in your brethren that are in the world" (1 Peter 5:8,9). The first part of this direction refers to the elements of personal character. What we are is of prime consideration in this conflict with the devil. Strong, good character is fully armed. Character is revealed in all our relationships, duties, and trials. But nowhere is character more telling than in our encounters with Satan.

We must be sober, calm, and collected—free from passion or intemperance. We must always be aware of spiritual dangers and deceptions. If we are vigilant, cautious, and active, we will never be surprised or overcome because of inattention or laziness. We must remain awake because of the full apprehension of the presence of a powerful, dangerous, and cruel foe. This is our strong defense.

James directs us to "resist"—to set one's self against the devil with will and thought, conscience and heart. We must hold the Word of God strictly, strongly, and rigidly. The truth of God inflexibly held will make one invincible to the devil, unyielding to his assaults. Temptation, toil, and affliction have been put upon God's saints in all ages. But it is by this warfare with the devil that we are perfected, established, strengthened, and settled.

"Be sober," says the apostle, for your adversary, the devil, walks about. This calm, self-collected condition, free from passion, and with the full mastery of all our powers, is essential to successful resistance of Satan. A passionate man is a weak man. A cool head and a calm heart are the conditions of successful warfare with the devil. The apostle adds the conditions of sobriety and vigilance. "Be vigilant," he says, watch, give strict attention, be cautious, be active. Vigilance awakens and sobriety arouses, giving us maximum strength.

### The Supreme Defense

The apostle James, in his frank, practical way, says: "Resist the devil, and he will flee from you." Resist means to set yourself against and make no concession to the enemy. We must meet the devil only to fight him, and we must talk with him only to withstand him. "Whom resist," says Peter, "steadfast in the faith." That is, be solid, firm, rigid in the faith. Be fixed in your beliefs, because the liberal person has no devil—only a very friendly one, and it does not fight against him.

If the spirit of forgiveness is always maintained

and constantly exercised, it is a supreme defense against the attacks of Satan. An unforgiving spirit is not only Satan's widest door into our hearts, but it is his strongest invitation and warmest welcome.

Paul urges a spirit of forgiveness as a barrier against the devil's entrance. Paul also hastens to close the door by his own readiness to forgive even in advance. "To whom ye forgive any thing, I forgive also: for if I forgave any thing, to whom I forgave it, for your sakes forgave I it in the person of Christ; lest Satan should get an advantage of us: for we are not ignorant of his devices" (2 Corinthians 2:11,12).

A spirit of forgiveness which is free from all bitterness, revenge, or retaliation has freed itself from the conditions which invite Satan, and it has effectually barred his entrance. The quickest way to keep Satan out is to keep the spirit of forgiveness in. The devil is never deeper in hell nor farther removed from us than when we can pray, "Father, forgive them; they know not what they do" (Luke 23:34).

## Your Chief Weapon

The devil is to be overcome. He is not only a hypocrite, full of quiet, slippery, and artful ways, but he is a man of war. He is a renowned warrior of many campaigns and many battlefields. His boldness and skill were tested in heaven. Angels were his enemies when heaven was the scene of his conflict and his defeat. Yet, he still fights. It takes strong young blood with fire and valor to meet him and conquer.

The devil must be defeated. Victory over him is victory all along the line. It takes strength and courage to overcome him. He is no coward, no disheartened enemy. The zeal and strength of mature faith is absolutely necessary in this battle.

The Word of God is the conquering sword in this warfare. The believer who has his quiver full of these divine arrows is swift, strong, penetrating and deadly to Satan and to sin. He will be more than a conqueror over the devil. The weapon used by the Son of God in His conflict with Satan was the Word of God, and by it He conquered.

"I have written unto you, young men, because ye are strong, and the word of God abideth in you, and ye have overcome the wicked one" (1 John 2:14). John, the apostle of love who was nearest the heart of his Lord, was full of this victory. John's love was too genuine to shrink itself into sickly sentiment or evaporate the devil into a mere influence. His experience was too profound and his memory too fresh for an impersonal devil or an impersonal Christ. John carried the scars of the battles with the adversary of his soul. He had witnessed the conflicts of many young soldiers. His soul had shared in their triumph and recorded their victories.

*Fight the devil and overcome him.* This is John's method of becoming fathers in spiritual power, rooted, grounded, and perfected. According to John, overcoming the devil is prerequisite to overcoming the world.

The mighty new-birth experience makes a man watchful like a sentinel at his post. When the enemy in power is massed in the front, the believer is like a watchman. He stands on the walls of the beleaguered city like a guard over a royal prisoner. This keeping and guarding himself is safety against Satan's inflaming touch.

The faithful, vigilant Christian keeps himself pure, and Satan comes and finds nothing in him. Every vantage point is barred and sleeplessly watched. "We know that whatsoever is born of God sinneth not; but he that is begotten of God keepeth himself, and that wicked one toucheth him not. And we know that we are of God, and the whole world lieth in wickedness (the evil one)" (1 John 5:18,19). "Keeping ourselves" is the surest pledge that Satan will not keep us.

## Satan's Greatest Fear

The martyrs who are faithful unto death, who love not their lives unto death, are victors in this warfare with the devil: "And I heard a loud voice saying in heaven, Now is come salvation, and strength, and the Kingdom of our God, and the power of His Christ: for the accuser of our brethren is cast down, which accused them before our God day and night. And they overcame him by the blood of the Lamb, and by the word of their testimony; and they loved not their lives unto the death" (Revelation 12:10,11).

The blood of the everlasting covenant must be sprinkled on the warriors who are victors against

Satan. They must have a clear, conscious experience of the saving power of that blood. They must have the ability to be a martyr and witness before any company at any cost. Their characteristics mark their devotion to Christ and their experience of His salvation. "He is mine and I am His" (Song of Solomon 2:16).

Satan cannot stand against a display of the blood of Christ. He turns pale at every view of Calvary. The flowing wounds are the signals of Satan's retreat. A heart sprinkled with the blood is holy ground on which he dares not tread. Satan trembles and cowers in the presence of the blood-sprinkled warrior.

Satan fears the power of that blood more than the attack of a legion of archangels. The blood is like the charge of an irresistible military force which destroys everything in its path. It is the blood applied and the testimony of its application that Satan fears. The martyr who is a witness of the power of that blood is more a barrier against Satan than a wall of fire. An experience of the atoning blood is heaven's infallible protection against Satan. Those in heaven overcame the devil in this way. We also "overcome him by the blood of the Lamb and the word of our testimony."

## Being A Servant

No sorrow is so pathetic as the sorrow of young widowhood. It is a sorrow exposed to Satan's attacks. Paul's direction puts widows on the defensive and guards them against the insidious attacks of the enemy. "I will therefore that the younger women marry, bear children, guide the house, give none occasion to the adversary to speak reproachfully. For some are already turned aside after Satan" (1 Timothy 5:14,15). No defense is more secure against Satan than a life crowned and crowded with unselfish duties. When they are faithfully done, the devil has no opportunity to speak reproachfully.

The devil's work is much helped or much hindered by the spirit of the servants of Christ. Gentleness is becoming to the servants of Christ not only as a beautiful adorning but as the foundation stone. Meekness and gentleness win men, for they imitate the Christlike character. Rudeness, impatience, and contention are not good recruiting officers for Christ.

"And the servant of the Lord must not strive; but be gentle unto all men, apt to teach, patient, in meekness instructing those that oppose themselves; if God peradventure will give them repentance to the acknowledging of the truth; and that they may recover themselves out of the snare of the devil, who are taken captive by him at his will" (2 Timothy 2:24-26).

## The Safest Place

*Watch* is the keynote of safety. The devil works on us with a thousand instruments, comes to us in a thousand ways, administers a thousand rebukes, and assaults by a thousand surprises. Watchfulness at all times is our only safety. We must remain wide-awake, not only when we see his form and fear his presence, but wide-awake to see him when he is not to be seen. We must repel him when he comes with any one of his ten thousand disguises—this is our wisest and safest course.

No cry of alarm is so frequent in the New Testament as the call to watch. No call hurts Satan so vitally or defeats him so readily as the call to watch. Being on the watchtower prevents all surprises and is essential to victory at all times.

The Son of God makes this call the keynote in many of His teachings. It is a call to be sleepless, to be vigilant, to be always ready. It is an image drawn from shepherds, in which we have Jacob's indignant defense and protest against Laban: "In the day the drought consumed me, and the frost by night; and my sleep departed from mine eyes" (Genesis 31:40).

To watch is to be opposed to all listlessness. It implies a wakeful state as if in the presence of some great danger. It is a cautious state untouched by any slumbering influence. Drowsiness and bewilderment are gone. It quickens us against laziness and spiritual sloth.

Read how the church at Sardis is called to the exercise of watchfulness. She was put to sleep by the dulling effects of a fancy church exterior and a proper religious structure. The Ephesian church is advised to combine watching with persevering prayer. The Corinthian church is urged to watch and stand fast. The Colossians are exhorted to "continue in prayer, and watch in the same"

(Colossians 4:2). The Thessalonians are to "watch and be sober" (1 Thessalonians 5:6).

Timothy, the young preacher, was to "watch in all things" (2 Timothy 4:5). Peter's call is "be ye therefore sober, and watch unto prayer," because the solemn end of all things was quickly approaching (1 Peter 4:7). Again he says: "Be sober, be vigilant; because your adversary the devil, as a roaring lion, walketh about, seeking whom he might devour" (1 Peter 5:8).

In Revelation we have the startling call, "Behold, I come as a thief. Blessed is he that watcheth, and keepeth his garments, lest he walk naked, and they see his shame" (Revelation 16:15).

The most frequent call to watchfulness is from our Lord. "Watch, therefore," He says, "for ye know not what hour your Lord doth come" (Matthew 24:42). Again He calls us to exercise this great grace, "Watch therefore, for ye know neither the day nor the hour wherein the Son of Man cometh" (Matthew 25:13). Again and again He calls us "to watch ye therefore."

The herald cry and the trumpet call from Him to us is to be awake—to be fully awake, to be tremendously awake.

"Watch ye therefore, and pray always, that ye may be accounted worthy to escape all these things that shall come to pass and to stand before the Son of Man" (Luke 21:36). "Watch and pray," He charged His disciples, and so He charges us to "Watch and pray, that ye enter not into temptation: the spirit indeed is willing, but the flesh is weak'' (Matthew 26:41). Still the flesh is weak, and watchfulness must always be united with prayer while we are in the flesh.

# Chapter Sixteen

# WEAPONS THAT WORK

*"Finally, my brethren, be strong in the Lord, and in the power of His might. Put on the whole armor of God, that ye may be able to stand against the wiles of the devil. For we wrestle not against flesh and blood, but against principalities, against powers, against the rulers of the darkness of this world, against spiritual wickedness in high places. Wherefore take unto you the whole armor of God, that ye may be able to withstand in the evil day, and having done all, to stand. Stand therefore, having your loins girt about with truth, and having on the breastplate of righteousness; and your feet shod with the preparation of the gospel of peace; above all, taking the shield of faith, wherewith ye shall be able to quench all the fiery darts of the wicked. And take the helmet of salvation, and the sword of the Spirit, which is the Word of God. Praying always with all prayer and supplication in the Spirit, and watching thereunto with all perseverance and supplication for all saints"*—Ephesians

Many prayers have missed the mark and been in vain because they were not combined with careful vigilance. There are many sad failures in Christian life because watchfulness failed. The devil's easiest target is a sleepy Christian. Many Christians have lost their souls because they failed to stay alert to Satan's attacks. Eternal vigilance is the price of political liberty. No less a price must be paid for our spiritual safety. The foolish virgins missed heaven because they failed in this virtue. Watchfulness would have brought them, along with the bridegroom, into the high joys of heaven's most celebrated hour.

In the sixth chapter of Ephesians, as stated above, the entire warfare with the devil and his legions is described. It also gives the sources of defense and victory. In this passage we have a view of the strenuous conflict and the battlefield on which the issues of eternity are tossed.

## Satan's Army

"For we wrestle not against flesh and blood, but against principalities, against powers, against the rulers of the darkness of this world, against spiritual wickedness in high places" (verse 12). The Christian's battle is with the devil and his methods. Satan's struggle is arranged with order, wisdom, and skill.

Principalities and powers are under his management and subject to his orders. They are his lieutenants, his prime ministers, his captain generals who carry out his orders and represent him fully. They are the world rulers with worldwide control and power. They master and control all the evil forces of the world. The devil and his high comrades are world rulers. Their might is as extensive as the world. Theirs is a fearful rule for evil, against the good and against man. Their subordinates, the rank and file, are innumerable and invincible, except to a God-equipped man.

What a vast and powerful array of aggressive, vicious, and cruel enemies. They are in heavenly places, the very place where Christ's power is located. This power is over us, above us, and around us. They are too mighty for us. Against this invisible, innumerable, all-powerful, and vast array, we *wrestle*. Wrestling is a close conflict. It is an intense and difficult conflict which tests all strength and strains every fiber. It is hand-to-hand, foot-to-foot, close contact.

This conflict is not with men, though men may give us much opposition in our Christian course. Our chief trouble and our great war is not with man but with all the mighty evil forces of the devil. It is a life and death struggle—a war for heaven and hell, for time and eternity.

## The Christian Soldier

The Christian must be a soldier by birth, by fortune, by trade. The most essential quality of a divine soldier is that he is not entangled "with the affairs of this life" (2 Timothy 2:4). The elements of self-denial, courage, and endurance are the vital characteristics of this military training.

Strength is the fruit of these high qualities. But it is strength far beyond his own strength. "Strong in the Lord, and in the power of His might" (Ephesians 6:10). In preparation for this war, the Christian soldier must look beyond himself. The strength of God, the very strength of God's almightiness, must be his.

The ability to stand, to fight, to conquer, and to drive the foe from the field will be found in God's armor. God's strength is imparted through God's armor. No power short of God can enable us to meet the devil. No partial equipment will suffice.

We are charged twice to make doubly sure to take the *whole* armor. We take God by taking His armor. We must make His armor our own. We put on God by putting on His armor—not outside but inside, not objective but subjective, not physical but spiritual. Christ made the armor, and the Holy Spirit puts it on us and makes it ours.

We have to fight through to the end, and having done all, to stand. We must first withstand and then stand. We gain and hold and then advance. Stand ready for the fight and stand in the fight.

## Truth And Righteousness

We must be strong for *the truth* in the inward parts. We are not imaginary soldiers fighting an imaginary war—all is real and true. Because he is truthful, a girded soldier is strong, prepared, and intense in his fight. Truth is the ornament of a

146

jeweled girdle, a diamond set in gold. We must conquer the devil by truth as the strength and support of our lives. We know the truth and have the truth because we have Christ who is the truth.

Heart righteousness makes head righteousness and life righteousness. We cannot fight without heart righteousness. The *"breastplate of righteousness"* protects the heart and makes us feel right. The old heart cannot be made right by the most skillful craftsman or by the most correct rituals. No tinkering on the old heart can make it right. It is as hard as a stone and crooked as the Jordan. No melting can make it soft, and no human effort can make it straight. We need a new heart soft as flesh and washed whiter than snow in the blood of Christ. A piece of Christ's heart—perfect, right, pure, and good—this is what is needed.

## Preparation And Faith

The feet must be shod with a *preparation* which is always ready to go, to do, and to suffer. This means no slow movements or reluctant doing of God's will. Being off guard creates a general unreadiness for life or death, for earth or heaven, for sacrifice or service, for doing or for suffering. It cuts the nerve of Christian valor and lays us open to surprises and crushing defeats. Always ready is the soldier's attitude of safety, and being ready to move precedes victory. Wakeful vigilance assures us of victory against the devil.

The *"shield of faith"* is the all-important and the all-covering piece of armor. The devil lets his fiery, poisoned darts fly. But faith catches them as they are directed at head or heart and quenches them.

Do you believe all victories are possible to the soldier who is valiant and strong in faith? There has never been a battle planned by hell's most gifted strategist which can conquer faith. All its flaming and terrible darts fall harmless as they strike against the shield of faith. "These all died in faith" (Hebrews 11:13). Faith made their death the crowning point. Faith brought to their dying hour the spoils of their victories.

## The Helmet And Sword

*"The helmet"* protects the head. Bear in mind that head-salvation and heart-salvation, real and full, are stronger than brass to protect the head. A heart fully saved holds the head firmly to truth and righteousness, as the anchor holds the ship in stormiest seas. "The *hope* of salvation," says Paul in Thessalonians, is the helmet. (1 Thessalonians 5:8).

The Christian soldier must put heaven strongly in his head and heart. He must see heaven, feel heaven, and keep heaven in the eye and in the heart all the time. He will stand with unsteady step if heaven seems far off. He will fight feebly if heaven is dimly seen. The full sight of heaven will give strength to his loins, zeal to his faith, glory to his future, and victory to the present.

The head will never be pierced while hope is its helmet. Nurture hope, strengthen hope, and brighten hope, for we are "saved by hope" (Romans 8:24). We must "abound in hope through the power of the Holy Spirit" (Romans 15:13).

*"The sword,"* the aggressive and powerful weapon, is the Word of God. The Spirit wields it and brings death to all our foes. The Word of God is our battlefield and victorious weapon. On it we stand and fight. With it we deal and defeat and ruin every foe. The Christian soldier is "not to live by bread alone, but by every word. . .of God" (Matthew 4:4). We cannot make too much of the Word of God. Christ foiled Satan with it. If we are to be valiant, true, and invincible, we also must have the Word of God dwelling in us richly.

The shield of our faith is the basis of our prayers and the essence of our girded truth. Head, hands, and hearts must be filled and saturated with God's Word; by it we live and by it we grow. It is our battle call and the sign by which we conquer. It is a glittering royal blade against all the assaults of Satan. *"It is written"* goes like steel to the heart of Satan.

As a weapon of defense and offense, God has magnified His Word above all His name. Those who are filled with God's Word are armed against all Satan's wiles and his devices. God's Word is "quick, and powerful, and sharper than any two-edged sword, piercing even to the dividing asunder of soul and spirit" (Hebrews 4:12). Satan feels it penetrating his joints and marrow, dissolving into weakness all his strength and making foolish all his wisest plans.

## The Weapon Of Prayer

The soldiers in the warfare against the devil must understand how to wear the armor of all prayer. The demand is for "all prayer" (Ephesians 6:18) at all seasons, in the intensest form, with a deep sense of personal need for God. Prayer must deepen and intensify into supplication. The Holy Spirit will help us into this kind of mighty praying and clothe us with this resistless power of prayer.

This intense conflict with the devil requires sleepless vigilance, midnight vigils, and a wakefulness which cannot be surprised. It also requires a perseverance which knows neither halting, fainting, nor depression. This kind of praying knows by clear spiritual intelligence what it needs. The prayer warrior knows the unlimited provisions that are available to supply all his needs. He knows the necessity of perseverance in prayer until the need is supplied and the provision is secured.

This kind of praying holds itself in loving sympathy with the entire family of God, making their conflicts, dangers, and needs its own. It is on the line of battle with the whole family of God. It takes on their enemies, their safety, and their dangers. "Supplication for all saints" (Ephesians 6:18) gives victory to every saint. The line of battle is one. Defeat or victory must come to all. The soldier fully equipped in God's armor is a veteran against the devil and invincible to all of his attacks.

It is not an easy thing to pray. Behind the praying there must lie the conditions of prayer. These conditions are possible, but they cannot be achieved in a moment by the prayerless person. They are always available to the faithful and holy, but cannot exist in a frivolous, negligent, and lazy spirit.

Prayer does not stand alone. It is not an isolated performance. Prayer is connected to all the duties of the Christian life. Prayer issues from a character which is made up of the elements of a vigorous and commanding faith. Prayer honors God, acknowledges His being, exalts His power, adores His providence, and secures His aid.

A skeptic would rationalize and cry out against devotion charging that it does nothing but pray. But to pray well is to do all things well. If it is true that devotion does nothing but pray, then it does nothing at all. The conditions of prayer are the sum of all the energized forces of practical working Christianity.

## The Power Of Prayer

Prayer brings God into the situation with commanding force. "Ask Me of things to come concerning My sons," says God, "and concerning the work of My hand command ye Me" (Isaiah 45:11).

We are charged in God's Word: "pray without ceasing" (1 Thessalonians 5:17); "in everything by prayer" (Philippians 4:6); "continuing instant in prayer" (Colossians 4:2); to "pray everywhere"

(1 Timothy 2:8); "praying always" (Colossians 1:3).

The promise is as unlimited as the command is comprehensive. "All things whatsoever ye shall ask in prayer believing ye shall receive" (Matthew 21:22). Jesus said, "Whatsoever ye shall ask" (John 14:13); "if ye shall ask any thing" (John 14:14); "Ye shall ask what ye will, and it shall be done unto you" (John 15:17); "Whatsoever ye ask the Father. . .He will give it you" (John 16:23).

If there is anything not involved in "all things whatsoever," or not found in the phrase, "ask anything," then these things can be left out of prayer. Language could not cover a wider range or involve more fully every detail of life. These statements are only samples of the all-comprehending possibilities of prayer under the promises of God to those who meet the conditions of right praying.

These passages, though, give only a general outline of the immense regions over which prayer extends its influence. The effect of prayer reaches and secures good things from regions which cannot be covered by language or thought. Paul exhausted his language and thought when he was praying. Still, he was conscious of necessities not covered, realms of good not reached, and of battles over enemies not conquered.

Paul covers these undiscovered regions by this general plea: "Unto Him that is able to do exceeding abundantly above all that we ask or think, according to the power that worketh in us" (Ephesians 3:20). The promise is, "Call unto Me, and I will answer thee, and show thee great and mighty things, which thou knowest not'' (Jeremiah 33:3).